# FROM FIRST ADAM TO LAST

# FROM
# FIRST ADAM
# TO LAST

## A Study in Pauline Theology

by
C. K. BARRETT, D.D.
*Professor of Divinity, Durham University*

Charles Scribner's Sons
New York

Printed in the United States of America
Library of Congress Catalog Card Number
62-19850

# THE HEWETT LECTURESHIP

WAS ESTABLISHED UNDER THE WILL
OF THE LATE WATERMAN T. HEWETT
WITH THE FOLLOWING STATEMENT OF PURPOSE:

'*I desire to place on record at the close of my life my profound faith in the Christian religion. I believe that the future of the human race and the highest individual character are dependent upon realizing in life, consciously or unconsciously, the spirit of our Lord and Master, Jesus Christ. Every successive generation must apprehend anew these truths, and a fresh statement of them by the ablest and most reverent scholars is desirable to secure their intelligent acceptance and recognition.*'

Mr. Hewett directed that the Fund should be administered by the President of the Faculty of the Andover Theological Seminary (now incorporated in Andover Newton Theological School), the Dean of the Episcopal Theological School, Cambridge, Massachusetts, and the President of the Union Theological Seminary, New York.

THE SCOPE OF THE HEWETT LECTURES IS DEFINED AS:

1. The truths of Christianity as shown in revelation, reason and history;
2. The value and authority of the Holy Scriptures and the influence of the Church in the world especially through Christian missions; and
3. The results of fresh discoveries in archaeology as bearing upon Christian truths.

SINCE ITS FOUNDING IN 1923, THE LECTURERS ON THE HEWETT FOUNDA-
TION AND THEIR PUBLISHED VOLUMES HAVE BEEN AS FOLLOWS:

1928 THE REV. CANON BURNETT HILLMAN STREETER, D.D.
'Primitive Church Order' (published in 1929 under the title 'The Primitive Church')

1932 THE VERY REV. PRINCIPAL ALEXANDER DUNLOP LINDSAY, C.B.E., LL.D. 18131
'Christianity and Economics' (published in 1933)

1938   THE REV. PROF. CHARLES HAROLD DODD, D.D.
       'History and the Gospel' (published in 1938)

1941   DR. RICHARD KRONER, PH.D.
       'How Do We Know God?' (published in 1943)

1946   PRES. FRANCIS CHO-MIN WEI, PH.D., L.H.D., D.C.L.
       'The Cultural Heritage of the Chinese and Christianity' (published in 1947 under the title 'The Spirit of Chinese Culture')

1947   THE RIGHT REV. GUSTAF AULÉN, TEOL. DR., D.D., BISHOP OF STÄNGNÄS, SWEDEN
       'Church Law and Society' (published in 1948)

1949   THE VERY REV. GEORGES FLOROVSKY, M.PHIL., D.D., S.T.D.
       'The Eastern Tradition in Christianity'

1955   PROF. OSCAR CULLMANN, DR. THEOL., D.D.
       'The State in the New Testament' (published in 1956)

1955   DR. ARNOLD TOYNBEE, D.C.L.
       'Christianity and the non-Christian Faiths in the Contemporary World' (published in 1957 under the title 'Christianity among the Religions of the World')

1959   DR. THOMAS F. TORRANCE, D.D., D.THEOL.
       'Theology and Scientific Method'

In March 1961 the Reverend Professor C. Kingsley Barrett, M.A., D.D., of the University of Durham, England, delivered a series of lectures on the Hewett Foundation at Andover Newton Theological School, Episcopal Theological School, Cambridge, and Union Theological Seminary, New York, under the title 'From First Adam to Last', which are published in this volume with some revisions and additions.

The appointees to the Hewett Lectureship are entirely free in the development of their themes, and the views expressed are not necessarily those of the Trustees of the Fund or their institutions.

# PREFACE

THIS BOOK, which attempts a fresh approach to some of the problems of Pauline theology, consists of the Hewett Lectures of 1961, delivered in March of that year at Union Theological Seminary, New York; Andover Newton Theological School; and Episcopal Theological School, Cambridge. The line of approach that I have followed is fully explained in the opening pages, and calls for no further explanation here. The main object of this Preface is rather to express my thanks, first to the Hewett Trustees, who did me the honour of inviting me to give the lectures, and secondly to all those who, in the three institutions I have named, welcomed me so warmly, entertained me so generously, and treated me as a friend and colleague. I do not, and shall not, forget their courtesy and kindness.

The chapters of the book reproduce the lectures substantially as they were delivered, though reconsideration, in part on the basis of conversations with my hearers, has enabled me here and there to make them clearer and more concise, and I have included all the passages that lack of time caused me to omit. The origin of the book in a series of lectures accounts to some extent for the disposition of the material, and also for the scale on which it is worked out. There is much that I should have liked to handle in greater detail.

C. K. BARRETT

Durham
October 1961

# CONTENTS

# ABBREVIATIONS

Bonsirven    J. Bonsirven, *Le Judaïsme palestinien au temps de Jésus-Christ*, Paris; Volume I, 1934; Volume II, 1935.

*Luke*    C. K. Barrett, *Luke the Historian in Recent Study*, London, 1961.

*Romans*    C. K. Barrett, *The Epistle to the Romans* (Black's New Testament Commentaries), London, 1957. (Harper's New Testament Commentaries), New York, 1957.

S.B.    H. L. Strack and P. Billerbeck, *Kommentar zum Neuen Testament aus Talmud und Midrasch*, Munich; Volume I, 1922; Volume II, 1924; Volume III, 1926; Volume IV, 1928.

*T.W.N.T.*    *Theologisches Wörterbuch zum Neuen Testament*, edited till his death by G. Kittel, since by G. Friedrich, Stuttgart, 1933– .

# FROM FIRST ADAM TO LAST

## I

## ADAM

THE title of this book, even when taken together with the headings of the several chapters, can scarcely be said to be self-explanatory. I therefore begin by explaining what I have in mind, and what I propose to do.

In the first place, though I do not doubt that there is in the book much that requires apology, I do not apologize for speaking of Paul. It is true that Paul cannot be said to stand in the middle of the New Testament picture at the present moment, and Pauline studies may be thought comparatively unexciting. There is today a new 'Quest of the Historical Jesus', and it would have been of absorbing interest (at least, to the writer) to enter into the post-formcritical situation, and to inquire why, if the gospels are not biographies, and do not provide us with material for constructing a biography of Jesus, those four men, Matthew, Mark, Luke, and John, made their work look so much like biography. This would provide a theme not only interesting but urgent. Alternatively, we might have turned not to the life of Jesus but to the other end of the century, and studied the Johannine and Lucan writings in order to find out what the developing Church made of the external pressure of gnosticism and the internal disruption of disappointed eschatology; we might have travelled a decade further still, and compared the alleged 'primitive catholicism' of Luke with the undoubted 'primitive catholicism' of Clement and Ignatius, and derived from the study interesting reflections on the limits and significance of the New Testament canon.[1]

These things might have been done, attractively and (more important) profitably. To deal instead with Paul is to run the

[1] There is a brief discussion of this question in *Luke*, pp. 25, 70-76.

risk of appearing merely to regurgitate the old Pauline and
deutero-Pauline clichés. If, however, we rightly understand the
questions that our colleagues are raising with regard to the life
of Jesus and the origins of catholicism (if that is the right word
for second-century Christianity) we shall see that Pauline
studies are, on account of these, not less but more important,
not less but more interesting. For, whatever the modern mode,
and the direction of recent studies, may be, Paul continues to
stand at the heart of the New Testament. As a man and a
theologian, I should be prepared simply to affirm this with
Luther, and to describe the Epistle to the Romans as the
'plainest gospel of all'. A historian, however, has more to say.
Paul is the one absolutely fixed point in early Christian history.
I do not suggest that we can know nothing at all of what Jesus
did and taught; but it is certain that all we do know about him
we know second-hand. We possess not a line of his own writing,
nor even any account of him written by an eye-witness. Again,
the Lucan and Johannine writings are obscured by literary and
historical problems too well known to require enumeration. It
becomes increasingly clear (though it is not undisputed) that
there was a gnostic problem in the first century, but not even
the documents discovered at Nag Hamadi have revealed to us
in their own words those men (for example) whom I John
shows us making their bold claim, I know him (ἔγνωκα αὐτόν.)
In any case, these Lucan and Johannine works lead us to the
edge of the New Testament period, and their authors touch
hands with the post-apostolic Church. Paul, however, takes us
back to the earliest period of Christianity, for his conversion
took place within a very few years of the crucifixion and resurrection of Jesus. His career is well known to us. If all copies of
Acts were obliterated we could still reconstruct from his own
letters a reasonably full account of his life and work, both as
Jew and as Christian. The same documents that permit us to
trace some of his actions, and to understand the psychological
processes that lay behind them, give us an unsystematic but
by no means incomplete summary of what he understood
Christianity to be. The Pauline corpus presents us with ex-

egetical problems enough (as we shall see); but historically and textually it stands as secure as any piece of literature, Christian, Jewish, or heathen, in the first century.

Paul thus provides us with an indispensable fixed point, a framework of reference. Whatever may be the final truth about Jesus Christ, and his own understanding of his person and his mission (and how often we are reduced here to hypothesis!), we *know* how Paul understood him in the forties, fifties, and sixties of the first century—and, we may add, in the thirties too, for there is no indication whatever that Paul radically changed his views of Jesus between his conversion and the beginning of his letter-writing; rather the contrary. Again, it may be that the Christians of the last two decades of the first century modified in significant ways the faith they received from their fathers; here too there is much scope for hypothesis and debate. But we *know* how Christianity was being preached and expounded in Ephesus, Corinth, and Rome, in the middle of the century. It is true that Paul was not the only Christian preacher and teacher of this period, and it is certain that his understanding of Christianity led him into controversy; this does not alter the fact that he is, at least, *one* fixed point, out from which we may move to various early deviations in faith, back from which we may, by means of the gospel tradition, work our way to Jesus, forward from which we may proceed to consider late first-century and early second-century developments. Paul remains the pole star for him who would navigate the waters of early Christianity.

In the second place, I must attempt to justify the way I have chosen to approach Paul's theology. Paul was not a systematic theologian, but he laid the foundations for systematic theology, partly by the unwearying mental vitality with which he worked at every problem he encountered in the course of his Christian activity and thinking, and partly through a natural capacity not merely for seeing both sides of a question but for holding them together, and at such a temperature that they became fused into a unitary scheme of thought. As such a theologian, he conceives a picture of God's dealings with humanity as a whole. These form a single story with an intelligible meaning, for it is the story of one person, God, who acts throughout with a consistent (though often mysterious) purpose. Paul's conception of this story and this purpose is sometimes described as a philosophy of history. There is truth in this description, for Paul does (though unsystematically) attempt to show the coherence of the historical process. The description is, however, inadequate, for it is not a rational coherence that Paul finds in history, but a personal and theological coherence. His system might in fact be described as the *reductio ad absurdum* of all philosophies of history:

> O the depth of God's wisdom and wealth and knowledge! How unsearchable are his judgements! How his ways baffle our attempts to track them down! (Rom. xi. 33).

Such an ejaculation, charged with deep feeling but expressing intellectual conviction, leaves room for only a very special kind of philosophy of history. For by this term a philosopher implies that he can find a unifying and intelligible principle within history, whereas Paul affirms bluntly that the only unifying and intelligible principle is outside history.

Alternatively, what Paul sets before us may be described as *Heilsgeschichte*.[1] This is an attractive term, and if it is carefully defined it can be applied to the Pauline system. It is not, however, completely satisfactory. The verse I have already quoted (Rom. xi. 33) sets a question mark against all theories of *Heilsgeschichte* which are capable (as some of them appear to be) of being represented on squared paper with the aid of co-ordinate axes. I shall not attempt here to deal with the question whether Pauline eschatology is or is not intrinsically capable of being reconciled with anything that can be called *Heilsgeschichte*. All that need be said is that the situation in which Paul conceived himself and his fellow-Christians to live was too complicated to be reduced to any simple straight line or curve. It was, and it was not, the age to come, since the resur-

---

[1] I know of no satisfactory rendering of this German word, and prefer, therefore, to allow it to stand. 'Redemptive history' suggests that history redeems, and 'history of salvation' suggests that salvation is an institution.

rection had already happened (in the person of Jesus), yet had not happened (for the rest of mankind). It would perhaps be possible to find a mathematical analogy to the Pauline dialectic, but it would not be a simple geometrical figure, and to use it would probably mean attempting to explain the obscure by means of the more obscure.

A second reason why the term *Heilsgeschichte* may be regarded as an inadequate account of Paul's view of God's dealings with men will bring us nearer to the plan of these lectures. Paul sees history gathering at nodal points, and crystallizing upon outstanding figures—men who are notable in themselves as individual persons, but even more notable as representative figures. These men, as it were, incorporate the human race, or sections of it, within themselves, and the dealings they have with God they have representatively on behalf of their fellows. Not that each member of the race may not and does not have his own relation with God; but these fall into a pattern which may be representatively described under a few names. These names follow one another in chronological sequence in the history books (in other words, in the Old Testament); but as far as the experience of mankind is concerned they need not be chronologically distinguished. Rather, they make up a dialectical pattern which provides the clue to Paul's understanding of mankind and of its history.

What I have just said can easily be applied to the names of Adam, Abraham, and Moses. One might interpret and fill out the assertion, 'Each of us has been the Adam of his own soul' (II Bar. liv. 19), by adding that all the names, Adam, Abraham, and Moses, in varying proportions and degrees, are descriptive of each man. It is not so easy to handle my fourth and fifth headings, 'Christ' and 'The Man to Come'—a phrase I hope to define more clearly when we reach it—because these are not only descriptive, or analytical, but also operative terms. I do not wish to anticipate now what I shall say in later chapters, except in so far as it may be necessary to correct a possible misapprehension. The transformation of the chronological sequence of Adam, Abraham, and Moses into a dialectical pattern may smack of 'demythologizing'—and I have no wish to exclude this process, still less to conceal my indebtedness to Dr. Bultmann. But it is necessary to add that Paul is far too mythological to be completely demythologized in this way. The plane of non-mythological anthropology is intersected by an event of which it is an essential constituent element that it happened at one time and not another, in one place and not another; and it is, according to Paul, to be so intersected again. These intersections are the events of Jesus, his coming in humiliation and his coming in glory; along with anthropology goes a Christology which in part is cosmological and mythological. Indeed, the names of Adam, Abraham, and Moses are christologically as well as anthropologically significant, and contribute to our understanding of Jesus; just as, conversely, it is in the last resort in the event of Jesus Christ that the truth about man, and thus about the 'typical' men, Adam, Abraham, and Moses, is revealed.

With so much of introduction we may turn to our first name—Adam. He is a difficult figure to handle, for two reasons. (1) A good deal of the material that might naturally and properly be used in this chapter could be, and must be, used also in the fourth and fifth, in which we deal with the last Adam. I must arrange it as best I can, asking my readers patiently to bear in mind that there is more to come. (2) Though some material that might be expected to appear in this chapter is thus omitted, other passages not containing the name of Adam must be included. Paul learnt to think in Hebrew, and knew that the name Adam ('ādām) means man. The result of this is not only an inevitable (even when subconscious) tendency to interpret the story of Adam anthropologically, but also that whenever in Paul we meet the word man (or other words, such as image, used in Gen. i-iii), we may suspect that Adam is somewhere in the background, characteristically hiding himself, though now behind the Greek language.

It is important to ask what Saul the Jew will have made of the figure of Adam. It is impossible here to add to, or even to survey, the vast amount of material bearing on this question that has already been collected by many scholars. If one sifts this material, it seems that nothing in the story of Adam impressed Judaism so much as the devastating punishment inflicted on him in his fall. This appears in many ways, most of them familiar, some of them naïve and amusing. Rabbinic literature abounds in references to the physical diminution and depotentiation suffered by Adam as a result of his and Eve's sin. His previous size, beauty, and wisdom were elaborated in order to stress the more forcibly the depths to which later generations of men had sunk. It is fundamentally the same picture, purged of its crudity and suitably hellenized in form and terminology, that is given by Philo,[1] whom I quote at greater length not because I think Paul more closely related to Hellenistic than to Palestinian Judaism but simply because Philo is both more quotable and more intelligible than the Rabbis, and yet proceeds from the same convictions. Here, as elsewhere, the differences between Hellenistic and Palestinian Judaism are less substantial than is sometimes supposed.

As a Greek Jew Philo sums the matter up in the words: This man truly was ὁ ἀληθείᾳ καλὸς καὶ ἀγαθός—the perfect gentleman (op. cit. 136). 'He was, it seems to me, perfect in either part of his being, both soul and body, and far surpassed those who came after him in his excellence in both respects' (ibid.). After demonstrating to his own satisfaction the high quality of the clay out of which Adam was made, and God's skill in making the first Adam 'most beautiful to behold', Philo adds that 'in soul also he was perfect' (op. cit. 138 f.). In this respect the first created man (of Gen. ii) was a copy of the archetypal man (of Gen. i), and 'the copy of a perfectly beautiful pattern must of necessity be perfectly beautiful. But the Word of God [or archetypal Man] is better than beauty itself (beauty as it is in nature), since it is not adorned with beauty, but is itself, to say no more than the truth, beauty's fairest adornment' (op. cit. 139). The first man was also the first cosmopolite, or citizen of the world, for to him only was the world both city and dwelling-place (op. cit. 142).

[1] See especially de Opificio Mundi, 135-52.

All this Philo develops at too great a length for us to follow him in detail. What I wish to underline is the turning-point in the story as Philo tells it. He says (*op. cit.* 151): 'Since none of the things that come into being is constant, but mortal things are subject to changes and vicissitudes, it was inevitable that the first man also should experience some misfortune.'[1] It is true that Philo goes on to point out that it was woman who proved to be the source of man's guilty life, but the accent continues to lie not on man's guilt, but on his misfortune. The presence of woman, Philo says, suggests bodily pleasure (*op. cit.* 152), and this entails wrongs and violations of law; yet once more Philo returns to his main point; the result of all is that men exchange an immortal and happy life for one that is mortal and unhappy.

I have used Philo as no more than a convenient illustration, a writer who is characteristic, and has the advantage of keeping to and developing his point as the Rabbis do not. It would be quite unjust to suggest that Jewish writers fail to regard the disobedience of our first parents as blameworthy; they do so regard it, and also underline Adam's reprehensible failure to show penitence for his misdeed. The point, however, on which they lay stress is not the sin but its consequences. These are not merely human but cosmic,[2] and as we go on to deal more fully with Paul's doctrine of redemption we shall be obliged to consider these cosmic consequences, for they lie behind the apocalyptic picture of a new age ushered in by an act of divine power in which evil forces are dispossessed and overthrown. The total result of Adam's revolt is that man suffers grievous misfortune. In himself, he is deprived of privileges and attributes which originally he enjoyed. He is mortal, not immortal; he is subjected to unhappiness, being the victim of fear, pain, and death; he is deprived of abilities, physical and mental, which were formerly his. Moreover, he finds himself in a

[1] Misfortune, κακοπραγία. At Wisdom v. 23 (not at Josephus, *Antiquities*, ii. 78, as is sometimes held) the word may mean 'evil-doing'; but this meaning occurs, so far as I know, here only. Elsewhere it means *misfortune, disaster*—such as that, for example, which befell the Athenians in Sicily (Thucydides, viii. 2).

[2] See W. D. Davies, *Paul and Rabbinic Judaism* (London, 1948), pp. 38 f.

world in which the sovereign authority of the beneficent God is manifestly denied. Evil powers are at large in the universe.

When we turn to the writings of Paul the Christian we find that this sense of disastrous consequences, both personal and cosmic, derived from Adam, is still present. They may be summed up in death, which is treated as almost a personal cosmic power. 'By man came death. . . . In Adam all die' (I Cor. xv. 21 f.). 'By the transgression of the One, Death reigned through that One' (Rom. v. 17). Other passages express the same truth slightly less distinctly; for example, 'The wage paid by sin is death' (Rom. vi. 23). Here too, however, the reference to the story of Adam is fairly clear: death is the punishment of sin, and of this the classic instance (and more than instance) is the story of Adam—man.

Death, however, though as far as man is concerned it is the last word, is not the only word. There is more evidence to be had. 'The creation was subjected to vanity ($\mu\alpha\tau\alpha\iota\acute{o}\tau\eta\varsigma$)'; it is eventually to be freed from 'bondage to corruption' ($\mathring{\alpha}\pi\grave{o}\ \tau\mathring{\eta}\varsigma$ $\delta o\upsilon\lambda\epsilon\acute{\iota}\alpha\varsigma\ \tau\mathring{\eta}\varsigma\ \phi\theta o\rho\mathring{\alpha}\varsigma$, Rom. viii. 20, 21). What is the origin of this but the pronouncement of Gen. iii. 17 ff.?

> Cursed is the ground for thy sake; in toil shalt thou eat of it all the days of thy life; thorns also and thistles shall it bring forth unto thee; and thou shalt eat the herb of the field; in the sweat of thy face shalt thou eat bread, till thou return unto the ground; for out of it wast thou taken: for dust thou art, and unto dust shalt thou return.

The same quotation from Rom. viii will take us a step further, for 'vanity' is not simply an abstract term, but denotes false gods, or evil spiritual beings.[1] We are familiar with the fact that for Paul the world was populated with principalities and powers, at war against God and against the true interests of men. Dr. G. B. Caird has brought out the connection in Jewish thought between the fall of the angels and the consequent fall of man under the authority of malignant spiritual beings, and the sin of Adam.[2] His point is made all the more cogent by

---

[1] See *Romans*, pp. 165 f.
[2] See *Principalities and Powers* (Oxford, 1956), pp. 67 f.

the observation (which I owe to Miss M. D. Hooker) that the rebellious beasts, no longer in subjection to man as in the original order of creation, became in time the source of the beast-like figures of the apocalypses, where animals represent spiritual powers. The fact that creation is out of hand not only makes agriculture hard work; it means the dominion of the astral powers.

A good illustration of this connection appears at the end of Rom. viii, where Paul refers to potentially evil powers which might be supposed capable of separating man from the love of God. True, they can never succeed in doing this, because God has triumphed, and will triumph, over them in Jesus Christ, the Lord; but Paul would not have mentioned them here if they had not been believed to constitute a serious threat. They are death, life, angels, principalities, things present, things to come, powers, height, depth. Of these, death is the immediate consequence of the fall, and life is perhaps best regarded as its rhetorical partner (though it is not in this context meaningless). Of the remaining terms, angels, principalities, and powers refer to spiritual powers of a kind not unfamiliar in Jewish literature. 'Things present' and 'things to come' are not simply present and future in a general sense, but refer to this age and the age to come—again technical terms of Jewish eschatological thought. 'Height' and 'depth' are technical terms in astrology, which is not characteristically Jewish. It is to be noted that the evil powers are connected both with the fall and with the movements of the heavenly bodies. There is evidence for the belief that these themselves had been disordered as a result of the fall.

There is a somewhat similar combination at Gal. iv. 8 ff. ; and I draw attention in passing[1] to the material in Colossians. In i. 16 it is said that thrones, dominions, principalities, and authorities have been created in, through, and for Christ. At i. 20 it is said that these powers have been reconciled through Christ, and at ii. 15 that Christ has triumphed over them (over principalities and authorities—the absence of the other words

[1] See a fuller discussion of Col. i. 15-20 below, pp. 83-88.

is not significant). It is clearly implied, though not specifically stated, that these beings had rebelled against their Maker and his Agent; the good creation had gone wrong, and an element in its perversion, which needed to be put right, was the revolt of spiritual powers and angels. Christ's triumph over them is a matter that must be considered later, in another context; there can be no question that it presupposes their antagonism.

Another passage to be studied is II Thess. ii. This chapter deals with the terrible events that must be expected before the *parousia* of Christ. Already the mystery of wickedness (τὸ μυστήριον τῆς ἀνομίας, verse 7) is at work; but worse things will come when restraining forces are removed and the mystery is revealed (ἀποκαλύπτειν). This revelation will take effect in a person who is described as the Man of wickedness, or the Wicked One (ὁ ἄνθρωπος τῆς ἀνομίας, ὁ ἄνομος, describing his character, verses 3, 8), and the Son of Perdition (ὁ υἱὸς τῆς ἀπωλείας, describing his end, verse 3). We need not here attempt to trace even in outline the history of Anti-Christ speculation. It is enough to note how the Wicked One expresses his wickedness. He regards himself as God, and consequently exalts himself over all the objects and instruments of human piety, so as even to take his seat in God's temple, claiming to be God. There can be no doubt whence this picture is derived; it goes back (whether directly or indirectly need not concern us; probably directly) to the oracle upon the Prince of Tyre in Ezek. xxviii.

> Because thine heart is lifted up, and thou hast said, I am God, I sit in the seat of God, in the midst of the seas; yet thou art man, and not God, though thou didst set thine heart as the heart of God; Behold, thou art wiser than Daniel; there is no secret that they can hide from thee. By thy wisdom and by thine understanding thou hast gotten thee riches . . . thine heart is lifted up because of thy riches: Therefore thus saith the Lord God: Because thou hast set thine heart as the heart of God; therefore behold, I will bring strangers upon thee. . . . They shall bring thee down to the pit; and thou shalt die the deaths of them that are slain, in

the heart of the seas. Wilt thou yet say before him that slayeth thee, I am God? but thou are man, and not God. . . .[1]

Undoubtedly the next step back from the Prince of Tyre in Ezek. xxviii is to Adam in Gen. iii. Adam, led on by his wife and through her seduced by Satan, succumbs to the temptation, 'You shall be like God' (Gen. iii. 5). In other words, as he takes the forbidden fruit he is in effect saying, like the Prince of Tyre, I am God—or, at least, I am as God, I am equal to God; whereas in fact he is man. There is one point that makes the contact between Gen. iii and Ezek. xxviii very close. The Prince of Tyre set his heart as the heart of God (Ezek. xxviii. 2, 6). Commentators rightly point out that 'heart' refers not to the emotions but to the understanding, and this view is confirmed by verses 3 and 4, which refer scornfully to the Prince's wisdom (ḥokmāh, ἐπιστήμη) and understanding (tᵉbūnāh, φρόνησις). But the tree of which Adam, against God's command, ate, was the tree of knowledge ('ēṣ haddaʿaṯ ṭōb wārāʿ, ξύλον τοῦ γινώσκειν καλὸν καὶ πονηρόν), and Eve perceived that its fruit was to be desired to make one wise (neḥmāḏ . . . lᵉhaśkīl, ὡραῖον . . . τοῦ κατανοῆσαι). Wisdom and knowledge play a special part in man's attempt to make himself God.

We cannot expect in such a context as this to be able to trace out a straight and simple line of development, either of literary forms or of personal figures. We are dealing with mythology, and moving in a dream world in which strange things happen without logical consequence or connection. But this at least is clear. Out of Adam, the man, grows a being whose essential nature it is that he denies that he is a man, and affirms his deity. Out of the father of the human race emerges (not by physical descent but by mythological development) the supreme enemy of those who, physically, must trace their descent from him. He is the enemy of man because he is the enemy of God, and he is the enemy of God because, being

---

[1] Cf. also the taunt against the King of Babylon in Isa. xiv. 4-21, especially verses 12-15. The parallel, however, is less close, and the oracle is in fairly close contact with the claim of the Babylonian kings to ascend *after death* to the mountain of the gods in the distant north.

God's creature, man, he has claimed to be man's Creator, God.

We began our treatment of II Thess. ii within the world of apocalyptical and demonological drama, and there is no question that Paul moves at ease (more easily than we) in that world. We have much to learn from his treatment of it, and it is doubtful whether the substance of what he has to say can be expressed without some use of mythological language. At the end of the paragraph, however, he moves on to a different line. In verses 9, 10 he speaks of the *parousia* of the Wicked One (ὁ ἄνομος). Before his destruction he will deceive those who are marked to perish, for he will be equipped with Satan's power to perform misleading signs and portents. This eschatology of woe is not simply futuristic ; it has in part been realized in the present.[1] In verse 11 Paul says that God is sending (πέμπει, present tense) a deluding activity (ἐνέργεια πλάνης) that men should believe what is false (εἰς τὸ πιστεῦσαι αὐτοὺς τῷ ψεύδει). Here he is speaking of what he has experienced in his apostolic work, and in terms similar to those of Rom. xli. 8, 25 (cf. I Cor. i. 23; II Cor. ii. 15; iv. 4); even when Christ crucified is placarded before men's eyes some will not believe; most remain under the influence of wickedness (ἀνομία), continuing, like Adam, and his descendant and successor the Man of wickedness, to think themselves equal to God and to insist upon occupying his place.

It is important to grasp what has happened here, for it will lead us to the next point. We begin with the myth of Eden, and the account of Adam's determination to supplant his Maker, thus denying the Creator-creature relationship which is the working basis of the universe. Creation is now perverted and subject to vanity; the reign of evil begins. For the moment we follow only one line of development. The prophet Ezekiel historicizes the myth which he has read or heard, applying it to the Prince of Tyre (in fact to the city itself—the Prince is only a representative figure-head, in whom Ezekiel shows no personal interest). The apparently impregnable heathen city in

---

[1] It must always be borne in mind that, for Paul, *both* the eschatology of bliss *and* the eschatology of woe are partially realized in the present.

its lawlessness and pride is marked down for destruction. The next step is that apocalyptic thinkers, of whom Paul was one, saw in the story a picture of the 'Man who went wrong', and thus under Satan[1] took the lead in the opposition to God which was at the same time the opposition to man-as-he-ought-to-be. It is an easy piece of demythologizing to see here the truth that man, whom pride so easily induces to push his way into God's place, is his own enemy, and it is a piece of demythologizing to which Paul himself points. He does not give up the belief that the apocalyptic warfare is to be waged; but he also brings it into the present, as the explanation of men's reaction to the Gospel. Those upon whom the deluding activity operates do not believe in the truth but approve of unrighteousness, and will be judged. Of believers it is said that God has chosen them as first fruits unto salvation in sanctification of the Spirit (a counterpart to the 'deluding activity', or $\dot{\epsilon}\nu\dot{\epsilon}\rho\gamma\epsilon\iota\alpha$ $\pi\lambda\dot{\alpha}\nu\eta s$) and belief in the truth. The difference between faith and unbelief is exactly the theme of the story of Eden. Men align themselves with Adam, the type of the Man of wickedness (as he is equally, though in a different sense, the type of the Son of man), or with God.

These observations lead us to consider the distinctive use Paul makes of the story of Adam. On the whole, his contemporaries, though not blind to Adam's guilt, tended to stress the misfortune suffered by men on account of the fall. This misfortune led to the apocalyptic presupposition that the world had fallen under evil powers, with the consequence that redemption is envisaged as taking place through a divine victory, which, in the defeat of the powers, undoes the evil effects of Adam's sin. Paul found no difficulty in thinking and writing in these terms, but they do not represent his only, or perhaps his most characteristic, way of dealing with the story of Adam; even when he is working in an apocalyptic framework, he edges his way out of it into a different pattern of

---

[1] II Thess. ii. 9 appears to distinguish the (wicked) Man from Satan: cf. Rev. xx. 10 etc. (the devil, the beast, and the false prophet). There is an analogy here with the relation between God and Christ, the (good) Man.

thought. Paul prefers to analyse the theological and anthropological significance of Adam's act. With this introduction we shall look at a few passages of outstanding importance.

Rom. v. 12-21: the paragraph sets out a detailed comparison (and contrast) between Adam and Christ, which is as relevant to the discussion of Christ[1] as to the present treatment of Adam. It lays great stress on the universal consequences of Adam's act; what these are we shall see presently. But it also casts light on the question what it was that Adam did. He sinned; but what is sin? It is evident from v. 14 that Paul saw something anomalous in the situation that prevailed between Adam and Moses. In this period there was no law, either of the simple Adamic kind ('Thou shalt not eat of it'), or of the immensely detailed and complicated Mosaic kind (the Pentateuch). Yet there was no accumulation of life on earth; men died—the distant descendants of Adam equally with their ancestor. Paul had already (v. 12) laid it down, in dependence on Gen. ii. 17, that death is the consequence of sin (cf. also vi. 23). This means (since death continued) that sin existed in this curious interim period; law is not necessary to the existence but only for the assessment of sin. Adam was thus guilty of an act that demonstrated a tendency to turn from God which was already in man—in man as he was, and as he is. How does sin take shape under the commandment?

The question is answered in a series of comparisons between Adam and Christ, and the actions of Christ enable us to work back (changing the signs, as it were) to what Paul supposed Adam to have done.

What Christ did is defined in terms of grace and gift ($\chi \acute{a} \rho \iota s$, $\chi \acute{a} \rho \iota \sigma \mu a$, $\delta \omega \rho \epsilon \acute{a}$, $\delta \acute{\omega} \rho \eta \mu a$), as obedience ($\acute{v} \pi a \kappa o \acute{\eta}$), and as an act of righteousness ($\delta \iota \kappa a \acute{\iota} \omega \mu a$). Its consequence was justification and life ($\delta \iota \kappa a \acute{\iota} \omega \sigma \iota s$, $\zeta \omega \acute{\eta}$). From these data it is not unreasonable to conclude—and Paul says so much—that the deed of Adam issued in death, and was marked by disobedience and by—the opposite of grace, that is by self-seeking, self-centred desire. It is in this way that Man (Adam) turns his back upon God and

[1] See pp. 69-72.

the way of life God created for him.

This analysis is confirmed in Phil. ii. 5-11—which also is as relevant to the discussion of Christ as to our present theme.[1] Again we may reason back from the work of Christ to the work of Adam; correspondence runs throughout the paragraph. To begin at the end, Christ is rewarded for his work by being made the head of all creation: to him every knee bows, of things in heaven, on earth, and under the earth. This recalls the fact that as a result of his sin Adam lost the lordship over creation he was intended to have, and became the subject of heavenly, earthly, and nether powers. Working backwards, Christ gained his title of Lord ($\kappa\acute{\upsilon}\rho\iota\sigma$) by his self-humiliation and obedience; he freely accepted the status of man ($\breve{\alpha}\nu\theta\rho\omega\pi\sigma$) and showed no anxiety to share the status of God ($\tau\grave{o}$ $\epsilon\hat{\iota}\nu\alpha\iota$ $\breve{\iota}\sigma\alpha$ $\theta\epsilon\hat{\omega}$). With this we must compare the story of Adam: at every point there is negative correspondence. Adam was not content to be the Son of man he was; the tempter's promise, You shall be as God, moved him to attempt self-aggrandizement by disobedience. Here, as in Rom. v, is a searching analysis of the theological and anthropological meaning of the fall—one might say, of its theological anthropology. Man's true existence is seen in the obedience and the exaltation of Jesus Christ, who freely accepts a subordinate relation to God, and through this reaches the dominion promised to man in creation ('Exercise lordship', $\kappa\alpha\tau\alpha\kappa\upsilon\rho\iota\epsilon\acute{\upsilon}\sigma\alpha\tau\epsilon$, Gen. i. 28). It is true that Jesus Christ exercises an additional lordship, over the rest of men; this is as the first-born among many brethren (Rom. viii. 29). Man's empirical existence we see in Adam. It is marked by a will-to-power, an impatience with a position suggesting any kind of inferiority. This will, this impatience are in a sense good—only because they are good can they be thought of as part of God's creation.[2] It was God's intention that man should 'exercise lordship' ($\kappa\alpha\tau\alpha\kappa\upsilon\rho\iota\epsilon\acute{\upsilon}\epsilon\iota\nu$), that he should be a lord

---

[1] See pp. 69-72.

[2] Cf. the statement of R. Nahman bar Shemuel that the evil $y\bar{e}\c{s}er$ (inclination) is very good (Gen. i. 31), because without it man would not build a house, take a wife, beget a child, or engage in business (Gen. R. ix. 9). See also p. 116.

(though a benevolent lord) over creation. The charter of man's existence is: Inferiority to God, superiority to all else in creation.

> Thou madest him a little lower than God ($m^{e'}a\underline{t}\ m\bar{e}{}^{'e}l\bar{o}h\bar{\imath}m$) . . . Thou madest him to have dominion over the works of thy hands; Thou hast put all things under his feet (Ps. viii. 5 f.).

Man's dominion must always be subject to the over-riding dominion of God, than whom he is always 'a little lower'; if he throws off the yoke of service to God he loses his own proper authority, with and for which he was created. It was by blurring the distinction between himself and God, by an attempt to place himself on equality with God and thus to secure that nothing should be excepted from his rule, that man fell.

There is another passage that throws light on our theme: Rom. i. 18-32. This has recently been analysed by Miss M. D. Hooker,[1] whose conclusions seem to me fundamentally correct. 'Paul's account of man's wickedness', she says, 'has been deliberately stated in terms of the Biblical narrative of Adam's fall' (op. cit. p. 301). The consequences of the fall are (a) idolatry, (b) sexual licence and perversion, and (c) wickedness in general. Idolatry, it is true, is not specifically mentioned in Gen. i-iii; but it may justly be said that it is from confusion of creation and Creator that idolatry springs. 'In listening to the voice of the serpent, Adam has not only failed to exercise his rightful dominion over creation, but, by placing himself in subservience to a creature, has opened up the way to idolatry' (ibid.); hence the partial and shadowy knowledge of God which is all that is left to man in place of the face-to-face communion for which he was created. The fall was not uncommonly connected by the Rabbis with sexual desire, and the Jewish suggestion that the serpent actually sought to seduce Eve (sexually) is probably reflected in II Cor. xi. Certainly the shame of Adam and Eve with regard to their nakedness, and their making of primitive garments, suggests that there is a strong sexual concern in the story. The chapter (Rom. i) issues

[1] In *New Testament Studies*, vi (1960), pp. 297-306.

finally in a more general list of sins which owes much to Hellenistic models; but it should be remembered that it was a commonplace of Hellenistic Judaism that idolatry was the parent of all kinds of moral evil.

In the passages quoted and referred to, Miss Hooker speaks of idolatry as a result of the fall. Elsewhere she suggests that the fall itself consisted in a lapse from God into idolatry.[1] The latter view is to be preferred to that which presents us with, first, a fall—undefined, save that it consisted in eating a forbidden fruit; and then, as a consequence of this, idolatry, sexual vice, and wickedness in general. In Rom. i, as elsewhere, Paul, though not unmindful of consequences, is even more deeply concerned with analysis. The 'consequences' are impressively introduced by the repeated use of the verb 'handed over' (παρέδωκεν).

> *Wherefore* (διό) God handed them over (verse 24).
> *For this reason* (διὰ τοῦτο) God handed them over (verse 26).
> *As they did not see fit* (καθὼς οὐκ ἐδοκίμασαν) . . . God handed them over (verse 28).

In each of these verses the 'consequence' introduced is essentially the same:

> Verse 24: the dishonouring of their bodies (τοῦ ἀτιμάζεσθαι τὰ σώματα αὐτῶν)—that is, sin, primarily sexual sin;
> Verse 26: dishonourable passions (εἰς πάθη ἀτιμίας)—again, sexual sin, especially sexual perversion;
> Verse 28: to do unseemly things (ποιεῖν τὰ μὴ καθήκοντα)—that is, all kinds of wickedness, including sexual.

Thus moral wickedness is the *result* of the fall: to eat an apple is not in itself morally good or morally bad, but from this non-moral act of Adam's morally bad actions flowed. The rest of the story, however, apart from the moral consequences, comes *within* the fall itself. This is borne out by the small insertions that separate the three pronouncements of sentence (παρέδωκεν

---

[1] 'The sin into which man originally falls is that of idolatry' (*ibid.*).

in verses 24, 26, 28). These are to be found in verses 25, 28a.
Thus

>   Verse 25: They exchanged the truth of God for a lie, and
>   worshipped and served the creation rather than the Creator
>   ... *for this reason* God handed them over (διὰ τοῦτο παρέδωκεν
>   ... ).
>   Verse 28: *As* they did not see fit to take cognizance of
>   God, God handed them over (καθὼς ...).

These verses show that the prior, non-moral but religious or
theological, fall consisted in a rejection of the knowledge of
God, an idolatrous turning from the Creator to the creature.
This is what the main passage, i. 18-23, says; and this (in Paul's
view) *is* the fall, not the consequence of it. Man was surrounded by the handiwork of God, his infinitely beneficent
Creator, who established him as lord over all his surroundings.
But having tasted dominion he sought to be free even of God,
and to extend his lordship upwards as well as outwards. He
thus refused to glorify God as his lord, and to give thanks to
him as the giver of all good things. This inordinate pride, the
perversion of a lordship that God himself had created for man,
was accompanied by the loss of man's knowledge of God, and
idolatry; that is, man's subordination to the creatures he should
have ruled. This subordination is elsewhere expressed in
apocalyptic-mythical terms, but here in moral terms, for man
proceeds to imitate the moral promiscuity of the beasts.

Two points in conclusion.

(1) It is clear that Paul believed that everything that could
be said about Adam as a (supposed) historical figure could be
said also about mankind as a whole; he took his Hebrew ('*āḏām*
—man) seriously. Adam was created by God for life; Paul can
say of himself (also representatively), 'Apart from law, I was
alive once' (Rom. vii. 9). The prohibition of desire (ἐπιθυμία:
the longing for something more and other than God himself
has provided) awakened in Adam, and (representatively again)
in Paul, the longing for all kinds of things (Rom. vii. 8:
πᾶσαν ἐπιθυμίαν). Rom. i. 18-23 is written in the plural; Adam's

refusal to recognize gratefully the sovereignty of his Creator is generalized into a like refusal on the part of all men. Not only for Adam but for all, 'Sin's wage is death' (Rom. vi. 23). Through the disobedience of the one man, the mass of men (οἱ πολλοί) were constituted sinners, and for all sin reigned in death (Rom. v. 18 f.; I Cor. xv. 21 f., 56). But how did Paul conceive the relation between Adam and mankind? There is no positive evidence in favour of a theory of seminal transmission; Paul does not say that all sinned *in* Adam (in Rom. v. 12 the Greek is ἐφ᾽ ᾧ), though he does say that all die in Adam (I Cor. xv. 22). Such a theory is not needed. Paul does not think of sin as a *thing* which, like an heirloom, may be handed down from father to son. Sin is a living, active, almost a personal, agency, and all sin needed was a means of entry into the race. Once this was found it did not need to be propagated—by sexual relations, or descent, or in any other way; it propagated itself. There is a sense in which each man becomes the Adam of his own soul,[1] though not the sense intended by Baruch, for no man begins with a clean sheet. Through the fall, each man finds himself in an inimical universe, under the dominion of usurping powers, of which sin itself is one; and, apart from the fact that these powers exercise dominion over him for their own ends, the inevitable and normal reaction of man in a dangerous situation is—self-defence. And this is sin, because its concern is with self, and not with God.

(2) Our study of Adam has sketched out the lines on which one of the most important questions relating to Paul's theology may be approached. When we consider the anthropological consequences of the fall it is natural to suppose that they can be remedied by anthropological processes. What man needs is to return to the true Creator-creature relationship for which he was made. He must abandon his arrogance, recognize the questionableness of all his deeds and thoughts, and submit himself wholly to God. In this way one arrives at an existential interpretation of Paulinism, in which there is much truth. This kind of interpretation is, however, inadequate, both because

[1] II Baruch liv. 19. Cf. p. 5.

it is not so easy as may appear to question one's existence and change one's relation with God, and also because it leaves out of account a quantity of Pauline material—not only what Paul says about the historical objectivity of God's act of redemption in Christ, but also the cosmic and demonic consequences of the fall, which lead to apocalyptic notions both of man's *malaise* and of his redemption. In other words, along with the existential interpretation of Paul there must be a cosmological (or apocalyptic-mythical) interpretation. I do not mean to suggest that these are independent of each other; but their inter-relation is a matter that must be deferred for fuller treatment below.

## II

## ABRAHAM

FROM Adam, we move through the pages of the Old Testament to Abraham; from myth, the representation of theological and anthropological truth in narrative form, to legend, the sort of story that is not unconnected with historical verity, that may be *ben trovato* even when not in the narrow sense *vero*, that clusters about notable men of the past (and present), and sometimes provides a personal point of crystallization for movements and tendencies. The change makes little difference to Paul. Myth moves from theology to narrative, legend from narrative to theology; in each, theology and narrative meet, and that is enough for him. The representative character of Abraham is naturally less clear and less universal than that of Adam; it is nevertheless sufficiently real. To Paul's Jewish contemporaries Abraham was both the father of Israelites and the first of proselytes; we shall see that Paul develops this thought, but he did not invent it.

Before, however, we come to the significance in the record of God's dealings with men that Paul attaches to Abraham, there are two negative points that deserve attention. I hope to show that they are not without positive interest and importance.

(1) When I was discussing the subject of this book with a learned friend he suggested to me (and the idea, though not his way of expressing it, had occurred to me also) that it might be interesting and profitable to include a chapter under the heading 'Absent Friends'. This is a true and valuable observation, and it would be possible to fill many pages with absentees, and with suggested reasons for their non-appearance. I can only allow myself space, at the beginning of this chapter, to mention two names, which might have filled the gap between Adam

and Abraham. On the first I lay no stress, and spend little time, simply noting it as possibly worth following up. It is Enoch. In the time of Paul there seems to have been a fairly considerable Enoch literature. It was the focus of much of the speculation about the Man, or Son of man, or Heavenly Man—a kind of speculation with which, if we may judge from the parallels in his letters, Paul was certainly acquainted. One might have expected him to draw on Enochic material; but he does not appear to do so. Neither the name of Enoch, nor any literary allusion to the Enoch books, can be found. This may be fortuitous; more probably it means that Paul's development of the thought of Jesus as the Man[1] was his own work, based perhaps on the Son of man material in the gospel tradition—an illustration of a fact we shall several times note, that Paul does not often take over ready-made material and apply it to Christ. He preferred to draw out his Christology from the Christ-event.

The second name I mention is both more interesting and more controversial—Noah. It is a datum of the concordance that the name Noah is not found in the Pauline epistles. Neither is there, so far as I can see, any allusion to the story of the flood and Noah's deliverance by means of the Ark, or the destruction of the greater part of mankind. It is possible that the word 'covenants' (accepting, as we should, the plural reading) at Rom. ix. 4 may refer, among others, to the covenant made by God with Noah after the waters had abated. The reference is possible but not necessary, and certainly is not emphasized; in fact it is better to suppose that Paul refers here to the three forms of the Mosaic covenant—at Horeb, in the plains of Moab, and by Mount Gerizim and Mount Ebal.[2] So far then we encounter silence. In particular, we encounter silence at one specially important place, where it might not be expected. We have already (p. 15) observed Paul's statement (Rom. v. 14) that death reigned—however anomalously—in the period between Adam and Moses, in which there was no law to make sin visible and assessable. Adam had received a specific command,

[1] See pp. 69-76.    [2] See *Romans*, pp. 177 f.

which he transgressed; but this command had no relevance to his descendants, who did not live in the Garden of Eden, and therefore had no access to the forbidden tree. Through Moses many laws were given—given to all mankind, as was believed, though only the Jews took upon themselves the yoke of the commandments. Between Adam and Moses there is no legal stepping-stone, and it follows that there was no law— μὴ ὄντος νόμου, as Paul says. What then of the so-called Noachian commands, given through Noah, and binding, as at least some Rabbis taught, upon all mankind, Gentiles as well as Jews? Do not these dispose of the lawless situation that Paul's argument presupposes? This is no simple question.

For one thing, it is far from easy to establish what, if anything, was believed by first-century Jews about the Noachian commandments. The rabbinic evidences[1] come from a later time, and this fact necessarily evokes a measure of doubt. It is, however, not on the rabbinic but on the Pauline side that the real difficulty lies. Could Paul have written as he does in Rom. v. 14 if he had believed that laws of universal applicability and validity had been given to all mankind in the persons of Noah and his sons? It is difficult to think that he could. This means that we must inquire further what becomes of the argument that in Rom. i f. Paul is dependent on this Jewish belief as the ground of his accusation that all men are responsibly guilty of transgressing God's laws. If Paul is not in these chapters using the concept of the Noachian commandments, what are his presuppositions?

This is not the place to attempt a full-scale exposition of Rom. i f., or an estimate of Paul's direct drawing upon Stoic ideas of natural law and the like, especially as I have had an opportunity of indicating elsewhere how I think these questions may be handled.[2] Here I simply make a general observation about the apostle and his methods. As I suggested in dealing with Enoch, it is his custom to go back to first principles rather than to take over ready-made conceptions, however helpful these might

---

[1] See, among other discussions, S.B. iii, pp. 37 f.
[2] See *Romans*, pp. 35-40, 49-53.

appear superficially to be. In this his instinct was right. Adam, whether we are thinking mythologically or existentially, provides a universally intelligible and universally applicable concept; Noah does not. Noah is the father neither of the race as a whole, nor of the chosen people. He represents adequately neither the universal natural law of the Stoics, nor the Torah of Moses. He stands between the two as an ultimately irrelevant figure.

This fact, that Noah has no real standing in the story of God's dealings with men, was unconsciously recognized in the rabbinic tradition too, for in one of the oldest forms, perhaps the oldest form,[1] of the tradition about the Noachian commandments it is said that these are seven in number, but that of the seven, six were given to Adam, only the seventh (the prohibition of Gen. ix. 4: 'Flesh with the life thereof, which is the blood thereof, shall ye not eat') being given to Noah, so that the so-called Noachian commandments are in effect Adamic commandments. In like manner, Paul in Rom. i f. deduces his views about universal obligation and responsibility from the place of man in creation; it is the fact that man is God's creature, and is related to God upwards and to the rest of creation downwards, that makes him answerable to God, not a set of legendary commandments.

Whether the 'apostolic decrees' of Acts xv reflect some primitive form of the Noachian commandments is a further question, and one that cannot be dealt with here, though it is a reasonable suggestion that the decrees represent an attempted compromise between the radical attitude to the law of the Pauline party, and the conservative wing, which intended to move from Judaism no more than it was obliged; and that this compromise was achieved by the adoption and Christianizing of the Noachian commandments. Perhaps it was in part for this very reason that Paul would have nothing to do with the decrees. The astounding paradox of the Mosaic law, which, being from God himself, was spiritual, holy, righteous, and good, yet had the effect of inducing sin, wrath, and death, and

[1] See S.B. iii, p. 36, and the evidence that follows.

had been superseded in Jesus Christ, was not to be set aside by Noachian legends. For every man, Jew and Gentile, the command of God is not minimal and compromising, but final and complete; for every man, the claim of God has been met in the universal Man Christ Jesus. There is no simple *via media*, or compromise.

(2) I come to my second negative point. In his recent book *Paulus*,[1] Dr. H. J. Schoeps deals at length with the theme of the Binding of Isaac (ʿᵃḳīḏaṯ yiṣḥāḳ), a theme to which he had already referred in an earlier work.[2] There can be no question that Judaism attributed great importance to the attempted sacrifice of his son by Abraham. The biblical narrative itself (Gen. xxii) is too familiar to require repetition. It was elaborated in various directions. Philo is probably pursuing a line of his own when he magnifies God's share in the birth of Isaac to such an extent as to call Isaac God's son, implying divine parentage (*de Mutatione Nominum*, 131); but it need not be said that both Abraham and Isaac were commanding figures in the Jewish world as a whole. In Gen. xxii the event is treated as a trial of Abraham's faith.

> Gen. xxii. 1: It came to pass after these things, that God did prove (*nissāh*) Abraham.

According to Jubilees, perhaps the oldest commentary, or midrash, on Genesis, the trial was prompted not by God himself, but by the chief of evil spirits, Mastema.

> Jubilees xvii. 16: And the Prince Mastema came and said before God, Behold, Abraham loves Isaac his son, and he delights in him above all things else; bid him offer him as a burnt-offering on the altar, and thou wilt see if he will do this command, and thou wilt know if he is faithful in everything wherein thou dost try him.

The story proceeds, and the result of Abraham's proved faithfulness is that 'the Prince Mastema was put to shame' (xviii. 12). Thus in Jubilees the obedience of Abraham (as in the Bible,

---

[1] *Paulus* (Tübingen, 1959), pp. 144-52.
[2] *Aus frühchristlicher Zeit* (Tübingen, 1950), pp. 229-38.

Isaac himself is passive) is the means by which the prince of evil is discomfited, though not finally.

In IV Maccabees, a laudatory account of the Maccabean martyrs, Isaac is referred to as an outstanding example of the martyr's readiness to lay down his life at God's command. This theme leads to a development in the original form of the narrative; Isaac himself comes to play a more positive part (see also below). Thus

> IV Macc. xiii. 12: Remember of what stock ye are, and at whose fatherly hand Isaac for righteousness' sake yielded himself to be a sacrifice.
>
> xvi. 20: Isaac, seeing his father's hand lifting the knife against him, did not shrink.
>
> Cf. xviii. 11: . . . Isaac who was offered as a burnt-offering.

It has been suggested, probably rightly, that it was to encourage faithfulness to Judaism, even at the cost of martyrdom, that reference to Isaac was introduced into the New Year service.[1]

Isaac came to be regarded not simply as an example of sacrifice, but as one whose sacrifice of himself had atoning efficacy. At times it seems to be quite forgotten that the sacrifice did not actually take place, and also that, so far as Gen. xxii goes, though willingness to sacrifice is certainly shown by Abraham, there is nothing to suggest that Isaac entered into the proceedings with equal readiness. There is a good collection of relevant passages in N. Johansson's *Parakletoi* (Lund, 1940), pp. 168 ff., from which I select as a clear, though not very early, example, Lev. R. xxix. 8 on xxiii. 24:

> If Isaac's children walk in transgressions and evil works, remember the binding of Isaac their father, and leave the throne of judgement and sit on the throne of mercy. Fill thyself with mercy for them, and have pity on them, and turn

[1] So Bonsirven, ii, p. 126, n. 1. It may be that we should mention here the puzzling verse, T. Levi xviii. 6: 'The heavens shall be opened, and from the Temple of glory shall come upon him sanctification, with the Father's voice as from Abraham to Isaac'. See M. Black, *Expository Times*, lx (1949), pp. 321 f. But this verse is probably a Christian addition.

for them the attribute (*middāh*) of judgement into the attribute of mercy.

Dr. Schoeps adds more material, but none which has the effect of bringing into the time of Paul the developed conception of Isaac as an intercessor, and of his sacrifice (or readiness for sacrifice) as a meritorious and atoning act. It would be wrong to say that such ideas are impossible in the early period. The idea of the atoning effect of martyrdom was current, and plays an important part in the New Testament; and (granted a little homiletical manipulation of Gen. xxii) it would have been as easy for Paul as for any other to bring Isaac within this orbit of thought. This possibility, however, is very far from being a demonstration that Isaac did provide, as it were, a ready-made category for the interpretation of the death of Jesus.

The crucial question is whether we do or do not find definite use of the (*ᶜᵃkīḏaṯ yiṣḥāḵ*) theme in the Pauline literature. Dr. Schoeps rightly refers to Rom. viii. 32: He did not spare (ἐφείσατο) his own Son, which recalls the language of Gen. xxii. 16, where God says to Abraham, Thou didst not spare (ἐφείσω) thy son. The verb in question (φείδεσθαι) is too common for us to build much on it; yet it is tempting to suggest not only that there is here a verbal allusion, but also that the parallelism runs a little further. In Romans the argument is that God who did not spare his own Son may be depended on to give us all things; in Gen. xxii, God, when Abraham did not spare his son, himself made all necessary provision. It will be noted that the Genesis passage does, the Romans passage does not, involve a change of subject; yet there remains some similarity, and there is a linguistic echo also, though not an absolutely convincing one. Can we go further? Dr. Schoeps (*Paulus*, p. 149) says that 'the fact that Jesus is given "up to death for our sins"', of which Rom. iv. 25; v. 8 f.; viii. 32; Gal. i. 4; I Thess. v. 10 and other passages speak, is very similar to Abraham's atoning sacrifice'. This seems to go a long way beyond the facts. In Rom. iv. 25 the relevant words are, 'he was given up on account of our transgressions'. The characteristic 'spare' ($\phi\epsilon\acute{\iota}\delta\epsilon\sigma\theta\alpha\iota$) is missing, but it must be remembered that the sentence occurs at the close of the chapter that deals with Abraham. This seems at first to strengthen the case for seeing here an allusion to the story of Abraham's son Isaac, whose birth has just been mentioned; in fact, however, it cuts the other way, for if Paul had had the $^{a}k\bar{\imath}\underline{d}\bar{a}h$ in his mind he could scarcely have written Rom. iv without making some plain reference to it. For him, the outstanding example of Abraham's faith was not his willingness to sacrifice his son but his confident belief that God would give him and his wife a child, notwithstanding their great age. The point of Rom. v. 8 ff. is different. In verse 8 it is the love of the Father of the given Son that is demonstrated, not his faithfulness or obedience; in verses 9 f. we read of the Son's death, not of the Father's giving him up. In Gal. i. 4 we read of Jesus Christ who gave himself for our sins. Here nothing forbids (though again nothing demands) the view that Paul is thinking of the $^{a}k\bar{\imath}\underline{d}\bar{a}h$, though in its developed form, for the biblical story is not in itself connected with the forgiveness of sins. I Thess. v. 10 ('who died for us') seems to be in no way specifically connected with Isaac.

Dr. Schoeps suggests that there may be a further trace of the Isaac story in Rom. iii. 25, when it is said that God set forth ($\pi\rho o\acute{\epsilon}\theta\epsilon\tau o$) Christ as a means of atonement ($\acute{\iota}\lambda\alpha\sigma\tau\acute{\eta}\rho\iota o\nu$). The suggestion is that in this expression 'set forth' recalls the $yir'eh$ (LXX, $\check{o}\psi\epsilon\tau\alpha\iota$) of Gen. xxii. 8. God promises through Abraham that he will himself provide ('look out') a lamb for sacrifice. Paul affirms that Christ is the sacrifice that God has provided. Dr. Schoeps recognizes that this suggestion strains the word $\pi\rho o\acute{\epsilon}\theta\epsilon\tau o$; and it would surely be unwise to press the analogy. It is more probably the Day of Atonement (if any particular Jewish liturgical act at all) that Paul has in mind here.

We are left with very little valid evidence. It seems (one cannot be certain) that there is a possible verbal allusion to the $^{a}k\bar{\imath}\underline{d}\bar{a}h$ in Rom. viii. 32—an allusion less definite than those to the Day of Atonement (Rom. iii. 25) and Passover (I Cor. v. 7). There is no reason at all why the parallelism between Isaac and

Jesus may not have occasionally presented itself to Paul's mind; but equally there is no reason to think that Paul ever developed the analogy, or used it in a serious exposition of the death of Christ. His silence rather forbids us to think that he did.

So far in this chapter our findings have been negative. Of Enoch and Noah Paul affords no trace; to the sacrifice of Isaac he makes at most a passing allusion. These facts suggest, what I believe to be both true and important, that Paul was not in the habit of taking over ready-made ideas and thought-forms, even when these bore a real affinity with his own thought. He preferred to work out his own material on first principles, and to pick out Old Testament characters for development on the basis of their intrinsic significance. But his first principles were given him in the Old Testament, and since in the Old Testament Abraham was an important figure it is not surprising that he is an important figure for Paul too.

What then does Paul make of Abraham? Like Adam, Abraham is a representative figure, important in his own right, and important also as ancestor, or type, of a group or groups. What we have to say about him must be taken under these two heads.

First, then, Abraham as a man. If Adam was a sinner, Abraham was a believer. In this word is summed up what Paul makes of the biblical story. It follows that, conversely, the figure of Abraham casts light on what Paul means by faith. The *locus classicus* is Rom. iv.

This chapter, which deals at length with the story of Abraham, follows immediately upon the paragraph (iii. 21-31) which contains the fundamental statement of the doctrine of justification by faith. Through the sacrificial death of Christ, God manifests his righteousness and justifies, not the virtuous and godly, but those who believe. This principle of God's action in grace avails for Jews and Greeks alike; it transcends the law, yet at the same time it establishes the law, in the sense that it is what the law—which is given through the Old Testament—really meant. Since the Old Testament is thus invoked, the question is inevitably raised, What of Abraham? It is often, and rightly, remarked in commentaries that we may suppose the case of Abraham to have been introduced by a Jewish adversary of Paul's argument, and it makes little difference whether we think of the Jew as an independent person, arguing with Paul from without, or as the Jew who was always present at the back of Paul's own mind. For Paul was certainly always aware of the high valuation that Judaism placed upon the person of Abraham. The material that illustrates this valuation is too familiar to be rehearsed in detail. In their different ways Hellenistic and Rabbinic Judaism depicted Abraham as the height of virtue and piety. In particular, though all the patriarchs had by their virtue and obedience to God laid up a store of merit (zākūt) on which Israel as a whole was able to draw, this was pre-eminently true of Abraham, who was pre-eminently 'our father'. There is a collection of rabbinic material, an indispensable foundation for the serious student to work on, in S.B. i, pp. 117-21. Within it I note two points, by no means universal in acceptance, yet common enough to suggest a background of public opinion. First: proselytes, who were not permitted to refer to Abraham as 'our father' (even after circumcision, in the synagogue liturgy they were obliged to substitute 'your father' for the 'our father' said by born Jews), could not draw on this store of merit. Secondly: there was a tendency to regard the benefits derived through Abraham as operating automatically along the line of physical descent. Thus in *Trypho*, 140 Justin alleges that the Jews suppose that 'the eternal kingdom will simply be given to those who are of Abraham's seed after the flesh (κατὰ σάρκα), even though they be sinners and unbelievers and disobedient to God'.

It is evident that Abraham must have acquired this out-standing treasury of merit, which was to be for ever at the disposal of his descendants, by a life of outstanding perfection, and by more than adequate obedience to God. Such a life he was believed to have lived. I quote only Kiddushin iv. 14:

We find that Abraham our father had performed the whole law before it was given, for it is written, Because that

Abraham obeyed my voice and kept my charge, my commandments, my statutes, and my laws (Gen. xxvi. 5).

This conviction was logically implied by the belief that
Abraham was a valuable source of merit, and it implied in turn
that Abraham, since he had done not merely all but more than
he was bidden, having kept the law perfectly, was justified
thereby, and justified evidently by his works. This conclusion,
if it could be sustained, would cut the nerve of Paul's argument;
there can be little doubt that this occurred both to him and to
his Jewish hearers. If, however, the inquiry touches the *justification* of Abraham there is a biblical text to consider which deals
explicitly with the issue; it is quoted not only in Rom. iv but
also in Gal. iii; we need not doubt that Paul had often debated
its meaning. Gen. xv. 6 runs as follows:

And he believed in the Lord; and he counted it to him for
righteousness (*wayyaḥš°ḇehā-llō ṣ°ḏāḵāh*),
LXX: καὶ ἐπίστευσεν᾽ Αβρὰμ τῷ θεῷ, καὶ ἐλογίσθη αὐτῷ εἰς
δικαιοσύνην.

Paul quotes in agreement with the LXX (apart from the initial
particle, and the spelling ᾽Αβραάμ[1]).

It was possible to understand this text in a way fatal to Paul's
argument. 'Faith' can mean 'faithfulness', the firm, upright
integrity of the religious man, who endures trial and temptation, and continues undeflected from the path of obedience.
This was the current interpretation: Abraham resisted all
temptations, and God himself was obliged to recognize the
result as righteousness. But is this really the meaning of the
text?

Paul has two ways of attacking this question. One is based
on technical exegetical methods.[2] Paul sees in the word *reckon*
(λογίζεσθαι) an opportunity of proceeding, by means of the

---

[1] It is interesting in passing to note the contrast with Philo, who is very
interested in the etymologies of the two forms of the name; unlike him, Paul
is not concerned to suck out of every detail the last drop of moral exhortation
and metaphysical deduction. Paul's use of the Old Testament is fundamentally
different.

[2] For details, see *Romans*, pp. 87–90.

device known as *gᵉzērāh šāwā'*, to Ps. xxxii. 1 f., where the same word is used. This parallel passage shows that the reckoning of faith as righteousness is equivalent not to the counting up of good works, but to the non-reckoning of sin, that is, to forgiveness. Paul next returns to Gen. xv. 6, and demonstrates that this non-reckoning, or forgiveness, took place while · Abraham was still uncircumcised; that is, was in an extra-legal condition. It therefore cannot rest upon perfect obedience to the law; faith is consequently a non-legal relation to God.

This argument, if one looks carefully into it, is much more than exegetical quibbling and playing with words. Serious theological issues are involved. It is, however, open to the objection that these isssues are not dealt with as seriously as they deserve, in that too much is made to hang upon verbal links. We turn therefore to Paul's second way of dealing with the question with which he is confronted. He analyses the religious and theological content of Abraham's situation, in much the same way that he handled Adam's. He does this twice, in Gal. iii and in Rom. iv; and in each place his argument touches closely another issue, which we are for the moment deferring —that of the relation between Abraham and his descendants, whether these are thought of as descended from his body (κατὰ σάρκα, as Paul would say), or as those who share his faith. This overlap may lead to a little repetition, and also to a measure of incompleteness in the present discussion; there is more to come later.

In Gal. iii we can for the moment confine our attention to verses 6–9. Paul has opened the debate with the simplest of pragmatical arguments. His Galatian correspondents are Christians—are manifestly Christians, since they have received the Spirit. This happened before there was any question of supplementing the Gospel with legal works. What point can there be in becoming circumcised when one has already received the Spirit? The gift of the Spirit is accompanied by the working of miracles: what more could one ask, what more could one expect, even if the law were imposed and kept? With this introduction Paul turns to Abraham. Evidently the question had been raised in Galatia in the form, Who are the seed, the children of Abraham? The Judaizers answered their own question: The marks of belonging to the family of Abraham are circumcision and the law. But, Paul answers, what is the criterion of righteousness, and thus the decisive element in the story of Abraham? See Gen. xv. 6: Abraham believed, put his trust in God. His children will be those who share his faith: It is those who depend upon faith who are the sons of Abraham (verse 7). This is confirmed by the terms of the promise made by God to Abraham: In thee shall all the Gentiles ($\pi\acute{\alpha}\nu\tau\alpha$ $\tau\grave{\alpha}$ $\check{\epsilon}\theta\nu\eta$) be blessed. Dr. J. Bonsirven has pointed out[1] that this universalist promise was neglected in the Jewish treatment of Abraham. 'It seems that the universalist promise, "In thee shall all the families of the earth be blessed" was scarcely ever taken up. The commentaries do not develop it; or else it undergoes this significant transformation—all the blessings that God bestows upon the earth, the rain, and even creation itself, were given for Abraham's sake.'[2] Paul, however, takes this promise as one of the decisive factors in interpreting the story of Abraham—another indication that in his treatment of Old Testament figures he goes back directly to the sources. Since Gentiles, who by definition stand outside the legal system, are to be blessed in Abraham, it follows that the blessing is not tied up with legal considerations. Abraham, in fact, as we have already seen pointed out in Rom. iv. 10, was a Gentile when God counted him righteous. It was not his circumcision or his obedience, but his faith that was the ground of his acceptance.

A glance through the rest of Gal. iii, which we are to study later[3] in another connection, shows that faith is connected with promise. A promise differs from a legal contract, which secures a return for services rendered; a promise implies a gift for which the recipient can make no claim, which he can never in any way secure for himself. It refers to something for which he can only trust the word that has been given him. In the measure

[1] Bonsirven, i, p. 76.
[2] See further Jewish interpretations on p. 40.
[3] See pp. 40 f.

in which he does trust the one who has promised the gift, he
is able to act on the assumption that the promised gift is as good
as his already. This line of thought, briefly set out in Gal. iii, is
dealt with more fully in Rom. iv. In the earlier part of this
chapter (especially in verses 4 f., 14, 16) it is brought out that
reckoning, promise, grace, and faith form a set of words which
belong together in mutual dependence.[1]

More detailed interpretation of Abraham's faith is given in
Rom. iv. 17-21, which must be quoted.

> . . . God, in whom he believed, God, who quickens the
> dead and calls into being the things which do not exist. This
> Abraham believed, hoping against hope, so as to become the
> 'father of many Gentiles' (according to the Scripture word,
> 'So shall thy seed be'). He considered without weakening
> in his faith that his own body was as good as dead (since he
> was about a hundred years old), and also the dead state of
> Sarah's womb. Looking rather to God's promise he did not
> waver in unbelief, but gave God the glory, was fully con-
> vinced that what God had promised he had the power also
> to do, and grew strong in faith.

Here Abraham's faith is specifically connected with the promise
that a son should be born to him, notwithstanding the old age
of both himself and his wife; that is, faith is response to promise,
a response that takes God at his word, and acts upon the assumption that his word is true and faithful. We may not un-
reasonably compare the position of Abraham with that of
Adam. Adam was placed by God in a situation which, on God's
own authority, guaranteed his life and future. This appears in
the verses which are at the same time promise and commandment:

> Be fruitful, and multiply, and replenish the earth, and
> subdue it; and have dominion over . . . every living thing
> that moveth upon the earth. Behold, I have given you every
> herb . . . and every tree . . .; to you it shall be for meat. . . .
> And God saw everything that he had made, and, behold, it
> was very good (Gen. i. 28-31).

[1] See *Romans*, pp. 88, 94 ff.

It was for Adam to take God at his word and live obediently and trustfully in the situation in which God had placed him, looking to God, as well he might, for the continued supply of all good things. This, as we know, Adam did not do. He doubted God's power and willingness to give him all that he regarded as good; he sought security for himself, and expressed this rebellious and self-seeking temper in an attempt to establish a wisdom and power-for-life that should make him independent of God.

Abraham found himself in a situation that appeared far less favourable. Instead of being placed within a 'promised land', a garden automatically supplying every need, he was summoned to cross the desert to an unknown country. He was given a promise, of life perpetuated in an enduring family, but he was given this promise in circumstances that, so far from favouring, plainly contradicted the possibility of its fulfilment. Wherever Adam looked, his eyes met instances of God's power and favour; for Abraham there was nothing but apparent denial of God's concern for him. Nevertheless it was Abraham who gave glory not to himself but to God, by recognizing that God truly was God, able to bring being out of non-being and life out of death; who took due account of all the unfavourable circumstances, yet remained confident that God could and would fulfil his word. Adam sought life for himself in defiance of God's way, and fell out of life into death; Abraham in a situation marked only by death placed the issue of life in God's hand, and received life. Faith, Abraham's faith, may thus be thought of as rebellion and disobedience, Adam's rebellion and disobedience, in reverse.

One might have thought that this reversal of man's first disobedience would result in man's final restoration. This was not so, for two reasons: (a) Abraham's faith (notwithstanding Jubilees and the discomfiture of Mastema[1]) did not put an end to the evil powers which had been admitted to the creation, and to authority within it, by Adam's unfortunate and blameworthy act; (b) although, as we shall see,[2] Abraham was a

---

[1] See above, pp. 26 f.        [2] See below, pp. 39-45.

representative man who had 'descendants', his faith was not
and could not be as universally effective as Adam's sin. Nevertheless, the contrast stands. Adam did not glorify God as God,
or give thanks to him (Rom. i. 21): Abraham did so. The un-
usual expression 'hoping against hope' (Rom. iv. 18) underlines this observation. In an entirely hopeful situation, Adam
did not hope in God, but endeavoured to secure his own future
for himself; in a hopeless situation Abraham hoped in God.

One more question must be handled before we close our
discussion of Abraham's own faith and consider him as an
ancestor, or representative. What is the relation between
Abraham's faith and his circumcision?

> Abraham received the sign of circumcision as a seal of the
> righteousness that came from faith, the faith he had while
> still uncircumcised (Rom. iv. 11).

Paul's argument that Abraham was on his side in the dispute
about justification and the law was open to a rejoinder; true,
Abraham was a believer while he was still uncircumcised—so
must every proselyte be at first, or he would never become a
proselyte at all, and Abraham the astrologer and idolater of
Ur was the first of proselytes; but, having become a believer
Abraham naturally and rightly took the next step, as a proselyte
must, of receiving circumcision. Current Jewish opinion connected Abraham's circumcision with Gen. xvii. 1 (Walk before
me, and be thou perfect), and drew the conclusion that only
with his circumcision did Abraham reach perfection. It would
follow that Gentile Christians, in Galatia and elsewhere, must
do as Abraham did, and perfect their faith by circumcision. Just
as Paul had to reinterpret Abraham's faith so that it was no
longer a religious work, so he had to reinterpret his circumcision (and not merely note its date, as he does in Rom. iv. 10).

Paul's language in Rom. iv. 11 must be understood on the
basis of Gen. xvii. 11:

> It (circumcision) shall be a sign (token) of a covenant
> ('ōṯ bᵉrīṯ; σημεῖον διαθήκης) between me and you.

This verse gives the meaning of the word 'sign'. The sign does not effect that which it signifies, but is merely a visible mark, pointing to a truth that exists independently. A Jew might look on circumcision as a token that he had a share in the covenant made between God and his people, but the fact might exist without the mark (as it did through most of Abraham's life) and was not dependent on it; nor did the mark in itself guarantee the fact, for Ishmael, who stood outside the covenant, was circumcised (Gen. xvii. 23).

It will be noted that Paul varies the language of Gen. xvii. 11. Instead of 'a sign of the covenant' he has 'a sign consisting in circumcision' ($\sigma\eta\mu\epsilon\hat{\iota}ον\ \pi\epsilon\rho\iota\tau o\mu\hat{\eta}s$, a different kind of genitive), 'the seal ($\sigma\phi\rho\alpha\gamma\acute{\iota}s$) of righteousness'. The use of the word 'seal' is not particularly important; it corresponds to the Hebrew ḥōṭām, which was not regularly, or early, applied to circumcision, and means little more than 'sign'. It does suggest also the idea of confirmation—the confirmation of something already existing. The most important parallel is I Cor. ix. 2; the Corinthian converts do not create Paul's apostleship; they are a visible token of something that exists independently of, and in fact created, them. In this sense circumcision is a seal of righteousness. Righteousness, however, is a word Paul has substituted in this context for covenant. Certainly Paul was aware of a covenant made between God on the one hand and on the other Abraham and his heirs—we have still to see what he makes of this in Gal. iii; but unlike his contemporaries he does not speak of circumcision as a sign of this covenant, perhaps because to do so would suggest (what is not implied in the Old Testament) that the rite was a requirement or condition preliminary to the making of the covenant, which would thus come to have a contractual character and be no longer an act of the free grace of God—in fact to be no longer a covenant in the biblical sense at all. The righteousness of which Paul is thinking here is not a visible righteousness consisting in just and holy acts and dispositions; it is a righteousness of relationship (between man and God), invisible in itself but capable of being testified to by an outward mark. The outward mark does not create righteousness (any more than the Corinthian Christians created Paul's apostleship), but only calls attention to its existence. It is at most a pointer to righteousness and, as Paul plainly says in Rom. ii, a very dangerous pointer at that, since circumcision of the flesh may be treated by men as a substitute for circumcision of the heart, with disastrous consequences, to which uncircumcision is greatly to be preferred.

Thus Abraham's circumcision was strictly parallel to his faith. His faith signified no human achievement but corresponded to the divine graciousness in quickening the dead and calling things that are not as if they were—in this case, calling righteousness into being. Neither faith nor circumcision was a work which could be regarded as laying a claim upon the opposite partner in an agreement.

So much for Abraham in his personal relation with God. We now turn to Abraham as a typical or representative figure. It is easy to do so, because the promise that Abraham received in faith was that he should become the ancestor of a very numerous family. At least, this is the part of the promise that Paul picks out.

> The father of a multitude of nations have I made thee (Gen. xvii. 5).
> All the nations of the earth shall be blessed in him (Gen. xviii. 8).

We should note also passages such as Gen. xxii. 18—

> In thy seed shall all the nations of the earth be blessed—

which refer to Abraham's family as the instrument or scene of universal blessing.

We have already[1] noted how these promises were handled in Judaism. Their universalist significance was minimized. Though from one point of view Abraham, who forsook the idolatry and astrology of Ur, and even called himself a proselyte (*gēr*, originally an alien, but in later Hebrew a proselyte), was pre-eminently the father of Gentiles, yet he was thought of not as the father of a multitude of nations but of one nation, and

---

[1] See above, p. 34.

the proselyte by saying not 'our father' but 'your father', was compelled to recognize this. Where the Abrahamic blessing upon all men was not generalized into a reference to monotheism or providence, it was weakened (*a*) by interpreting the Hebrew (perhaps rightly) to mean that Abraham would be a standard of blessing—a father, for example, might say to his son, May you be as fortunate as Abraham, and (*b*) by the view that the blessing was to be had only by becoming a proselyte.

Paul's own treatment of the subject we may study first in Gal. iii. We have already looked at verses 6-9, where Paul moves from one quotation (Abraham's faith counted to him as righteousness) to the second (the blessing of the Gentiles). These are brought together: the blessing of the Gentiles is that God will justify them by faith. Since to be 'of faith' is to be justified, and since justification is the root of all blessing, and since Abraham was justified by faith, it follows that (in the words of verse 9), those who are 'of faith' (οἱ ἐκ πίστεως) receive the blessing along with believing Abraham. Paul, however, is not content simply to make this affirmation over against his Judaizing opponents. He counter-attacks. So far from being blessed, those who depend on works of the law (are ἐξ ἔργων νόμου), even born Jews, are under a curse. This point is carefully argued in verses 10-14. The law itself pronounces a curse upon every one who does not continue in and perform all the things written in the law. To this the Judaizer would reply: True: and this means that I escape the curse, and you, Paul, receive it, for I insist upon the whole law, including circumcision, and you notoriously do not. No, Paul retorts, for see Hab. ii. 4, where it is written, He that is righteous by faith shall live (ὁ δίκαιος ἐκ πίστεως ζήσεται); faith (πίστις) is declared by Scripture to be the condition of man's righteousness and life, and faith has nothing to do with the law, which is based upon its converse, doing.[1] It follows that no man does continue in and perform all the things written in the law, and that the law thus has the effect of imposing a universal curse,

---

[1] The occurrence of ζήσεται in both Hab. ii. 4 and Lev. xviii. 5 is a very important step in the argument. It forms a sort of *g<sup>e</sup>zērāh šāwā'* (see p. 33), by which the putting together of the two passages may be justified.

from which the only way of escape is in the fact that Christ (as witnessed to by the law itself) has taken the curse of the law upon himself in the death he died. This was in order that the promised blessing, which includes the gift of the Spirit, might come to the Gentiles, through faith, and in Christ (verse 14). This conclusion leads Paul back to the promise made to Abraham and to his descendants. The expression used several times over in the biblical narrative is the collective noun 'seed', in Hebrew zeraʿ, in Greek σπέρμα. Paul underlines the choice of this word in verse 16:

> He does not say, And to thy seeds (σπέρμασιν), as with reference to many, but as with reference to one, And to thy seed (σπέρματι).

The promise thus made, like a will,[1] cannot be altered or added to by any third party; it must stand until the appointed heir comes to take possession. Now the 'seed' is, Paul affirmed, Christ. It is in him that the curse is resolved, and it is in him that the blessing is realized. The end of the story is reached in verse 29; those who belong to Christ are Abraham's seed, and are thus heirs in terms of the promise.

It will be seen that this argument turns upon the fact that the Old Testament promise is made to Abraham *and to his seed*, and the identification of the 'seed of Abraham' with Christ. Christian believers become heirs of the promise not by works of the law, nor by imitating Abraham's faith, but by the faith through which they are joined to Christ. Naturally, this is not very different from the faith that Abraham had; it too rests upon the power of God to raise the dead. This leads us back to Rom. iv.

Here, too, Paul is aware that the story of Abraham as an individual is incomplete. It was told for our benefit (verses 23 f.), and Paul quotes another Old Testament verse to show the connection between Abraham and the Gentiles (Rom. iv. 17; Gen. xvii. 5). He does not, however, speak of the covenant, and his brief allusion to a verse containing 'seed' follows a line

---

[1] Paul's word, διαθήκη, means both testament and covenant.

quite different from that of Gal. iii—the seed (it is implied) are to be numerous. The essential point is that men should share Abraham's faith. It is in this way that Abraham becomes the father of both Jewish and Gentile Christians: Gentiles imitate the faith he had while still, like them, uncircumcised, and Jews imitate the same faith which was still the essential matter even when Abraham was circumcised. Again, there is a close resemblance between Abraham's faith and that of Christians; indeed, it is the same faith, since it is directed towards the God who raises the dead. The last two verses in Rom. iv bring us back in full circle to Gal. iii. Abraham's faith was counted to him for righteousness; if we have the same faith we may expect the same forgiveness of our sins, the same reckoning of righteousness. Yet this is no automatic process, depending simply upon an inward change in man and in his attitude to God. Paul's last words in the chapter speak of Christ who was delivered up 'for our sins', and raised up 'for our justifying'. Thus it is through Christ that Christians become sharers in Abraham's faith; this is not far from the statement that it · is as Christ's property that men become the seed of Abraham, and heirs in terms of the promise.[1]

It will be clear that neither in Romans nor in Galatians is Paul concerned with a relation to Abraham based simply upon physical descent. The Jew may indeed be one of Abraham's children—if in addition to having Abraham's blood in his veins, and sharing his circumcision, he also follows in the footsteps of Abraham's faith. The Gentile may equally be a child of Abraham—if, notwithstanding his lack of circumcision and of blood-relationship, he has faith. Either will be of the seed of Abraham if he belongs to Christ; and in Christ there can be neither Jew nor Greek (Gal. iii. 28). This point is explicitly made in Rom. ix, and made so clearly that it scarcely needs exposition.[2] It arises in Paul's painful questioning of the fact that Israel as a whole has rejected the Gospel. Can this mean that God's promises to Israel have failed? No—if you consider what the term Israel really means. It must not be interpreted in

[1] See also pp. 76-79.  [2] See *Romans*, pp. 180-183.

terms of physical descent from the patriarchs. It is not all those
who are physically descended from Abraham that are counted
as children of Abraham. In this argument two points come
under consideration, election and promise. Not election only,
or Jews would be able to reply, Yes, we are descended from
Isaac, not Ishmael, therefore we are truly the seed of Abraham;
but promise also, for Isaac was born, unlike Ishmael, not of an
ordinary union between man and woman, but as a result of
the creating, promising word of God. Isaac was the child, on
God's side, of promise; on Abraham's, of faith. Whether Paul
knew the saying, 'God can of these stones raise up children
for Abraham', we cannot tell; we can be sure that he would
have approved of it.

True, there was a continuing family of Abraham, produced
by a natural sequence of births. This was Israel after the flesh,
and Paul himself belonged to it.[1] But what was the place of
this apparent Israel in the purpose of God? Was it nothing but a
hallucination, a deception? This would not be true. The physical
line of descent from Abraham and the patriarchs was not in
itself identical with God's election, and Israel after the flesh was
therefore not identical with the 'Israel of God' (Gal. vi. 16).
Yet Israel after the flesh in the vicissitudes of its history and the
personal religion of its members, was always present to act as a
pointer, more or less clear, more or less accurate, to the veritable
purpose of God. There is an analogy to this in Paul's treatment
of circumcision in Rom. ii. The whole passage seems at first
to be in confusion. Circumcision is, and circumcision is not,
profitable. The fact is that circumcision of the flesh may, and
also may not, point to circumcision of the heart. If it is regarded
as an end in itself, as something which of itself is able to
guarantee man's relation with God, it is a lie and a blasphemy.
If it is taken as a denial of itself, a pointer to the fact that outward
rites are worthless, and worse than worthless, in relation to God,

---

[1] Paul can even call this Israel, the seed of Abraham. He himself is 'of the
seed of Abraham' (Rom. xi. 1), and so are the Jewish Christian apostles
(II Cor. xi. 22). This is conventional language, and Paul easily slips into it,
without meaning to deny his theological apprehension and assessment of the
situation.

if it leads man to trust not in himself but in God, to offer not one member but the whole of his *ego* to God, then circumcision is a very profitable thing. Similarly, descent from Abraham may be understood as a constant reminder of the electing grace of God, and it is so understood by Paul, who had it 'as though he had it not'. It may, however, for those who cling to it (whereas Paul had sacrificed it—Phil. iii. 7) and use it for their own ends, become a blasphemy.

This appears in the last passage we shall study, the allegory of Gal. iv. 21-31. This passage is beset with many difficulties, including textual problems, which cannot be dealt with here. In verses 22 f. Paul sums up the biblical narrative. Abraham had two sons. The first was Ishmael, the child of the slave Hagar. The second was Isaac, the child of the freewoman and lawful wife, Sarah. We learn later that Ishmael persecuted Isaac; this statement rests on Gen. xxi. 9, as often interpreted at the time. So far we have narrative; but these things are ἀλληγορούμενα, deeper truths set out in secret form. The two women are two covenants. Hagar is one, namely that from Sinai, based on law; she bears children for bondage. How Paul connects Hagar with Sinai we need not now discuss; the essential point is that he does make the connection, and adds that Hagar-Sinai corresponds with empirical Jerusalem, the headquarters of Judaism, and is in bondage yet, as are all Jews (except Christians). Sarah represents a different covenant, that of God's promise to Abraham; she represents the eschatological Jerusalem, now in heaven but waiting to be revealed. This is the mother of Christians, who, being, like Isaac, children of promise, are free. They are persecuted now by their half-brothers, but they will nevertheless prove to be the true heirs.

The allegory acknowledges that in this age Judaism has all apparent right on its side. It has the present (νῦν) Jerusalem as its centre; it is in a position to persecute dissidents, and to impose itself and its will. It claims to be the child of promise, the legitimate descendant of Abraham, and there is no evident means of disproving its claim. But the truth is given away by the fact that it has become entangled in the law, and thus is liable to slavery. It has become (cf. p. 43) a subtle imitation, but in truth a standing denial, of that true descent from Abraham, which is a matter of grace, election, promise, and faith.

Viewed in himself, Abraham could be the last term in the series that began with Adam. Adam sought to establish his own security at God's expense, and lost it. Abraham was content to leave his security to God, in faith, trusting in the power of God to bring life out of death. So far, this was a reversal of Adam's fall. It is also true that Abraham's faith may be imitated and repeated. Yet Abraham is not the end of the story. His faith did not reverse the total situation created by Adam's fall, but being part of that situation was itself immediately perverted, so that Abraham's descendants, instead of being a people relying solely on God's call, election, and grace, came to imitate not their father but Adam, and to try to establish their own security in terms of their physical descent. The legitimate issue of Abraham, through Isaac, became illegitimate, because they were perverted by the fact that, in Adam, they belonged to a perverted universe; the illegitimate issue of Abraham, through Ishmael, became (or some of them became) legitimate, because, in Christ, they belonged to a restored universe.

# III

## MOSES

I BEGAN the chapter on Abraham with a reference to 'absent friends'. No one could place Moses in that category; his name (not to consider mere allusions) is mentioned nine times, against only five for Adam. Moreover, in one of the most important of the passages that deal with the sequence we are considering, Rom. v, he is mentioned along with Adam and Christ as marking one of the three great turning-points in the history of the race. Not even Abraham is named here: only the command to Adam, and his disobedience; the law given through Moses; and righteousness and life through Christ. Moses is certainly no absent friend. At least, he is not absent; whether he is a friend or no is a question we shall have to consider.

Yet, ought he not to be one of the absentees? Why does he appear in Paul's story? This may seem a stupid question, but we are encouraged to ask it by the fact that Paul himself does so. We have already glanced through Gal. iii, and this chapter, added to references made elsewhere to Adam, seems to make a clear, connected, and complete story. Man ('ādām) has abused his place in the world. He has brought the universe under the control of the demonic powers that now dominate men's lives, and placed himself under the power of sin and death. There has been a preliminary and partial reversal of this melancholy situation through Abraham. In the first place, God made a promise of blessing which should remove the curse, and that for all nations. In the second place, Abraham accepted this promise in a faith which was the reverse of Adam's disobedience. It is true that the process was not completed in Abraham as a historical figure: the terms of the promise include a reference to his 'seed', which means Christ; moreover, though

46

Abraham's obedience may be said in a sense to deal with the anthropological problem created by Adam it does not deal with the cosmological problem;[1] that is, it does not include the overthrow of the spiritual powers of evil—witness the way in which the 'seed of Abraham' is immediately perverted to mean the opposite of what it should mean.[2] We therefore know that the story cannot end with Abraham; but this does not lead us to expect an entirely new figure, Moses, to intervene between Abraham and the birth of the promised 'seed', especially since this new figure appears (at least, at first sight) to mark not an advance towards the goal of the complete restoration of humanity, but a set-back—a set-back because he brings commandments, and we know what was the effect of a commandment upon Adam, and because he suggests a nationalist approach to questions that are of universal significance.

It is precisely this question that Paul himself raises in Gal. iii. The covenant (διαθήκη) with Abraham resembles, he says, a testament (διαθήκη) made and duly ratified by a testator. It is well known that no other person has the right to set such a testament aside, or to add a codicil to it. It must stand as it is. What then, on this analogy, can intervene between Abraham, to whom the promises were made, and the 'seed' in and through whom they were to be realized? Τί οὖν ὁ νόμος; Paul asks—Why then the law? Or, to paraphrase his question, What is Moses doing in this interval?

At first sight, Moses is an otiose figure. But certainly he is a great man. He is one of the primary authorities, perhaps the primary authority, of the Old Testament. A quotation may be introduced by the simple formula, Moses writes (Rom. x. 5). Apart from his significance as legislator and biblical author, Paul has important stories to tell about him.

The most important perhaps is the midrash on events in the story of the Exodus, contained in 1 Cor. x. The setting is an argument against the rash folly of the Corinthians, who suppose that, because they are fortified by the sacraments of

[1] See pp. 20 f.        [2] See pp. 44 f.

baptism and the Lord's Supper, they may safely take part in heathen festivals without falling under the sway of the demons who take advantage of such rites. In fact, the sacraments afford no such *ex opere operato* protection, as the analogy of Israel in the wilderness shows.

> All our fathers were under the cloud, and all passed through the sea, and they were all baptized ($\dot{\epsilon}\beta\alpha\pi\tau\dot{\iota}\sigma\alpha\nu\tau o$) into Moses in the cloud and in the sea. And they all ate the same spiritual food, and they all drank the same spiritual drink, for they drank of the spiritual rock that followed them; and the rock was Christ. Yet with the greater number of them God was not pleased, for they were laid low in the wilderness (1 Cor. x. 1-5).

Their destruction was due, Paul adds, in dependence on the Old Testament narrative, to their idolatry and immorality. They had their sacraments, but they were not thereby automatically protected against sin and its consequences. Let Christians in Corinth beware.

The origin of this midrash is a question of some interest. According to Lietzmann[1] it was produced by Paul, who used the methods of Hellenistic Judaism; according to Dr. Jeremias[2] it was based upon an already existing Palestinian product. We need not take sides in the dispute. Undoubtedly there is Palestinian-Jewish material that points towards the midrash as Paul gives it to us. For example, the Old Testament nowhere says that the Fathers were *under* the cloud; but we have evidence that the Rabbis found exegetical means of developing out of the one cloud of the Old Testament, two, four, seven, and even thirteen clouds, so arranged that the Israelites were completely surrounded by cloud, and hence were under the cloud. Again, Paul's statement that Israel passed *through* the sea is not strictly in accordance with the narrative of Exodus, the main point of which is that the Israelites passed over dry-shod. The Rabbis, however, contribute the picture of the sea forming up like a

[1] H. Lietzmann, *An die Korinther I, II* (fourth edition, supplemented by W. G. Kümmel; Tübingen, 1949), p. 44.
[2] J. Jeremias, *Zeitschrift für die neutestamentliche Wissenschaft*, 28 (1929), pp. 314-19. See Kümmel's note in Lietzmann-Kümmel, *op. cit.* pp. 180 f.

railway tunnel through which the Israelites passed, so that they may be said to have gone *through* the sea. There is also in rabbinic sources a good deal of material about the rock from which the children of Israel drank. How much of this was already in existence (as Dr. Jeremias thinks) as a biblical argument (otherwise wanting) for the baptism of proselytes, it is impossible to be certain. There is little positive evidence for this conclusion, but two arguments are adduced in favour of it. (1) Paul seems to assume that his point will be immediately taken up, without the necessity of explanation. He must therefore have believed that what he was saying was familiar. This is not a very strong point; Paul is apt to make jumps in his argument, and makes considerable assumptions with regard to the knowledge of his readers. How much did his Corinthian readers know of the Old Testament, to say nothing of Palestinian midrashim? (2) A second argument is based on the fact that Paul uses the middle voice of the verb 'to baptize'. This is not the voice that would be expected if Paul had in mind the common Christian terminology, where the passive is natural; but it is the voice that would be used of Jewish baptism, which was self-administered. This is a stronger, but not conclusive argument. The Greek middle is not a reflexive; and for Christian usage we may compare Acts xxii. 16 and I Cor. vi. 11. Nevertheless, it should probably be allowed that part at least of the midrash was of Jewish origin; it would be rash to describe it as Palestinian rather than Hellenistic, since Hellenistic Jews had good reason to be interested in proselyte baptism.

It is thus unlikely that Paul made up the midrash as a whole; for one detail, however, he is almost certainly responsible. He says that the Fathers were baptized 'into Moses', εἰς τὸν Μωϋσῆν. It seems to be impossible either to parallel or to explain this phrase on the basis of Jewish sources. It can only be accounted for as based upon the Christian baptismal formula, 'into Christ'.[1] For this addition, then, with its specific and honorific reference to Moses, Paul himself was responsible. It

---

[1] Which therefore ought not to be explained on the basis of the present passage! See Lietzmann, *ad loc.*, and J. Jeremias in *T.W.N.T.* iv, p. 874.

was he who decided that it was reasonable to parallel 'into Christ' with 'into Moses'. In the new, Christian situation baptism is *into* Christ; that is, into his possession and under his authority, so as to be incorporated into him and to share in him the transference from the old age of sin and death into the new age of the resurrection. The comparable figure in the story of the first exodus from bondage to freedom is Moses; Israelites were in a sense incorporated into him. Paul goes on to say (I Cor. x. 6) that these things have become examples for us (τύποι ἡμῶν), and (verse 11) that they happened to the men of old 'so as to provide examples' (τυπικῶς). These verses do not mean that there was a precise equivalence between Moses and Christ, since, though the Fathers are said to have been baptized into Moses, they drew their spiritual drink not from Moses but from Christ himself, with whom the rock was identified (verse 4). Rather, Paul is drawing a general parallel between the situation and events of the Exodus, and the situation and events with which he has to deal in Corinth.

That Paul saw a *relation* between Moses and Christ is undoubtedly true. It would, however, be rash to describe this relation as 'typological' in any precise sense of the word. In this context at least, Paul's word (τύπος) means not 'type' but 'warning example' (see above). There is no need to press the evidence; as it stands, Moses occupies a lofty place.

A second passage that glorifies Moses (though in a limited degree) is II Cor. iii. Again, a well-known Old Testament narrative is presupposed. According to Exod. xxxiv. 29-35, when Moses came down from Mount Sinai after speaking with God and receiving the two tables of the law, his face shone. He himself was unaware of this, but Aaron and the people saw it and were afraid to approach him. Moses called them, and they came near; he then handed on to them God's commandments. After he had spoken to them he put a veil on his face, and remained veiled until he returned to speak with the Lord; he then took off the veil until he came out, when he spoke again to the children of Israel and they saw his shining face. Then he put on the veil once more till he should return to speak with God.

There are features of II Cor. iii which it is not easy to harmonize with this story; Paul's interpretation of it seems to have distorted some of the facts. Verse 7 follows the Old Testament narrative closely enough with the addition, however, of one significant word. The children of Israel were not able to gaze upon Moses's face because of the glory shining in it, which glory *was being done away* (τὴν καταργουμένην). This corresponds with the statement in verse 13, that Moses put a veil on his face so that the children of Israel might not gaze upon the end of that which *was being done away* (τοῦ καταργουμένου—what this is, is not made clear; the gender shows that it is not simply the glory (δόξα) that is referred to; cf. verse 11). In Exodus nothing is said of the vanishing or fading of the glory, and it is not lack of boldness (as II Cor. iii. 12 f. implies) that leads Moses to veil himself, but simply consideration for those who cannot bear to look upon the supernatural. Clearly, Paul is not developing his own doctrine out of the Exodus narrative; he knows what he himself has to say, and uses figures and imagery drawn from the Old Testament to give it vividness and force, though it is also true that he sees in the Old Testament story positive truth, of which he learns the full meaning, not in the Old Testament itself but in Christ. Our task is to reconstruct the working of Paul's mind, and in the light of this to see what he makes of the figure of Moses.

There are two sets of data. The first is the Old Testament story, which recounts a transfiguration of Moses. Philo had already fastened on this and developed it, for the greater glory of the lawgiver:

> He descended far more beautiful in appearance than when he went up, so that the beholders were astonished and terrified, and were no longer able to direct their eyes towards the approach of the sun-like beam that shone forth from him (*de Vita Mosis*, ii. 70).

Communion with God, and the dignity of his office as lawgiver, bestowed on Moses a glory that was apparent in his face, and intolerable to ordinary men, in consideration for whom

Moses after a time put on a veil which, however, he removed when he returned into the presence of God. It will be noted that Philo says nothing of the fading of the glory; the glory persisted, and for that reason men could not continue to look at it.

The second set of data is more complicated. Paul knows that the law, and the covenant inaugurated on the basis of it, great as they are, are nevertheless in process of being done away.[1] The transient glory of the law has been superseded by a greater glory, the glory of Christ (the ὑπερβάλλουσα δόξα of II Cor. iii. 10), and the old covenant (verse 14) by the new. The new covenant is based, not upon a written law, but upon the work of the Spirit; its issue is not condemnation and death, but justification and life. Its progress, however, has not been as easy and triumphant as might have been expected. The children of Israel themselves, who should have welcomed it, have, Paul knows, in fact rejected it (Rom. ix. 2, 31; x. 1-3; xi. 7-10). The rejection will not be permanent; in due course Israel will turn to the Lord and be saved (cf. Rom. xi. 11, 26).

These Christian data have modified the Old Testament story. Moses remains a figure of glory, but instead of exalting his glory, as Philo and the Rabbis do, Paul minimizes it. In fact, however, it is not so much the Old Testament story as the current Jewish interpretation of it that Paul modifies. The only negative feature that he introduces is, as we have noted, the statement that the glory on Moses' face was passing away, and this, though not contained in the Exodus narrative, is not flatly contradicted by it. Exod. xxxiv. 33 (cf. verse 35) simply states that when Moses had finished speaking with the people, 'he put a veil on his face'. This *could* have been because the glory was fading, though this is contrary to the spirit of the narrative. Undoubtedly it is in contradiction with the rabbinic belief that the glory still lingered in Moses' countenance even after his death, just as the assertion that the law brings condemnation

---

[1] Note Paul's use of καταργεῖν in relation to the law, at, *e.g.*, Rom. vii. 2. τὸ καταργούμενον at II Cor. iii. 11, 13 is the whole religious system based on the law.

and death is in contradiction with the fundamental Jewish conviction that it brings righteousness and life.

It is very probable that Paul has modified the story in the light of his belief that the law was 'done away' in Christ. Here, however, as always in Paul, the 'abolition' of the law is not a complete negation, still less a condemnation. Between the old dispensation and the new there is parallel as well as contrast. As Dr. J. Jeremias has pointed out,[1] in II Cor. iii, Moses is treated as a figure not of Christ, but of Christian ministers, such as Paul himself. Indeed, for Paul, the key-word both in the Old Testament narrative as he tells it, and in the Christian parallel he lays beside it, is ministry.[2] The Corinthians are an epistle of Christ ministered ($\delta\iota\alpha\kappa\omega\nu\eta\theta\epsilon\hat{\iota}\sigma\alpha$) by us' (iii. 3). iv. 1 takes up the main line of thought with 'Since we have this ministry ($\delta\iota\alpha\kappa\omega\nu\acute{\iota}\alpha\nu$)'. The intervening section develops the theme of Christian ministry, which is a veiled manifestation of the glory of God, and so can be both compared and contrasted with the 'ministry ($\delta\iota\alpha\kappa\omega\nu\acute{\iota}\alpha$) of death and condemnation' (verses, 7, 9) through Moses. But the veil that obscures the true meaning of the law is now described as lying not upon the face of Moses, but upon the heart of his (Jewish) hearers (verse 15); that is, the fault, the failure of the mission, the obscurity or veiledness, lies not with the law itself—which is good; cf. Rom. vii. 12, 14— but in the circumstances of a fallen race, dominated by sin. If only this veil is taken away—and the Spirit can remove it (verses 16 f.)—Israel will turn to the Lord.

This involved passage does contain a glorification of Moses, but it is a paradoxical glorification, which points onward to the meaning Paul found in the law of which Moses was the mediator. It is a striking fact that Billerbeck could observe, 'In the old rabbinic literature we have met with no passage in which reference is made to the veil of Moses in Exod. xxxiv. 33 ff.' (S.B. iii, p. 516). The veil, however, is essential to Paul's understanding of the story, and of Moses himself. It is not

---

[1] *T.W.N.T.* iv, pp. 873 f.
[2] $\delta\iota\alpha\kappa\omega\nu\acute{\iota}\alpha$; not 'ministry' in the modern technical sense, but the service of the Church to God, performed, though in differing ways, by all its members.

through the law of Moses, which remains inextricably entangled in veils, but through the Gospel that men may, with
unveiled face, behold in a mirror the glory of God.[1]

These two passages, in I and II Corinthians, are important,
especially in what they hint at and then deny. With a little
alteration, both could be made to speak of Moses (as Stephen
does in Acts vii. 35) as sent by God to be a prince and redeemer
(ἄρχων καὶ λυτρωτής). In I Cor. x he is at the same time the
deliverer who leads his people through the desert and across the
Red Sea, and the dispenser of baptism, and of spiritual food and
drink. His people are baptized into him, so as to become one
with him, his property, and his obedient subjects and devotees.
In II Cor. iii he is an almost supernatural being, a θεῖος ἀνήρ,
whose face is resplendent with divine glory. There seems to
have been in Paul's time a tendency to make of Moses just such
a divine, cult figure. There is a vivid illustration of this in the
synagogue frescoes at Dura-Europos. So far as they touch our
subject they may be described in the words of M. Rostovtzeff.[2]

> I am inclined to accept [the interpretation] of Professor E.
> Goodenough, and to see in these figures the representation of
> four decisive moments in the life of Moses: Moses and the
> burning bush, Moses on Mount Sinai, Moses reading the
> scroll of the Law, and Moses after his death surrounded by
> the sun, moon, and stars. Moses is presented here somewhat
> in the character of one of the great founders of new religions
> of the ancient world, as a canonized and almost deified hero,
> founder of the Jewish religion; a counterpart in some degree
> of Buddha and Christ. The idea is uncanonical. The semi-
> divinization of Moses is stressed by the square nimbus which
> surrounds his head, light in the pictures which show him
> living, black in that which shows him after his death.

On this subject, as on many others, Philo has no single clear-
cut pronouncement, but his various, by no means harmonious,
statements are significant of a general atmosphere. For him,

---

[1] Reasons for taking κατοπτριζόμενοι in this way (and not as 'reflecting as
in a mirror') are given in Lietzmann-Kümmel, op. cit. pp. 113, 200.

[2] Dura-Europos and its Art (Clarendon Press, Oxford, 1938), p. 108.

Moses is a king of divine appointment, a king who is at the same time lawgiver, priest, and prophet (*de Praemiis et Poenis*, 53 f.). The theme is worked out at greater length in *de Vita Mosis*, ii. 1-7, as follows:

It is a king's duty to command the things that should be done, and to forbid those that should not; but to command the things that must, and forbid the things that must not, be done, is the proper function of law, whence it follows immediately that the king is a living law, and the law a righteous king. But one who is king and lawgiver ought to keep in view not only human but divine affairs, for without God's oversight the affairs of kings and their subjects do not go aright. For this reason such a one [as Moses, the king and lawgiver] needs the supreme priesthood. . . . But since to this king, lawgiver, and high priest countless matters both human and divine were unknown . . . he must needs also attain the gift of prophecy, in order that by the providence of God he might discover those things which cannot be perceived by reasoning. For prophecy reaches to those things which the mind fails to grasp. . . .

Thus equipped, Moses was the ideal king, of God's own choosing,

not like some of those who thrust themselves into positions of power, by weapons and instruments of war, by forces of cavalry, infantry, and navy, but on account of his virtue and goodness, and the kindness to all men, which he was always wont to show (*de Vita Mosis*, i. 148).

The origin of these notices we need not inquire into; it will suffice to say that the parallels that have been found in Egypt, and among Stoics and Neo-Pythagoreans, are substantial. Philo was an eclectic, and not least in his treatment of Moses as the ideal king, who united under his sceptre religious and civil legislative functions.

Philo has more to say about Moses. There is at least superficial evidence in favour of the view that to him Moses was the founder of a cult. Thus

Moses pitched his own tent (Exod. xxxiii. 7) outside the camp, outside the whole bodily organization ($\tau o\hat{v}$ $\sigma\omega\mu\alpha\tau\iota\kappa o\hat{v}$

παντὸς στρατοπέδου), that is he established his mind (γνώμην) where it could not be moved, and so began to worship God. He entered into the darkness, the invisible region, and remained there, being instructed in the most sacred rites. So he becomes not only an initiate but also a hierophant of the mysteries (ὀργίων), and a teacher of the divine truths which he will impart to those whose ears are purified (de Gigantibus, 54).

The language of de Cherubin, 49, is even plainer:

I myself was initiated under Moses, the beloved of God, into the greater mysteries, but when I saw the prophet Jeremiah, and knew him to be not only initiated but a worthy hierophant, I did not hesitate to resort to him.

These descriptions of Moses are important, but they must not be allowed to lead us too far. They mean less than they appear to mean at first sight. What Philo thought of the mystery cults we know; he believed them to be bombastic and pernicious nonsense. In the passages quoted he is as usual exercising a journalistic philosopher's right to take up any language without regard to its total implications if only it serves its turn for the moment. Long ago Reitzenstein[1] argued, with much force, that there was an Egyptian-Greek philosophical custom of adopting 'mystery' language for purposes which were intended to be impressive without having anything to do with mysteries in the strict sense, and Philo may have adopted this convention.

If Philo was cautious, however, there were others who were dashing, and the figure of Moses was brought into the border-country between Judaism and Hellenism, and indeed over the frontier into heathenism and magic. The evidence is scanty, for there were many to suppress it, but it is sufficient to indicate several stages, or forms, of Hellenization.

The Jewish poets Ezekiel and Demetrius introduced Moses into their works harmlessly enough. The surviving fragments (in Eusebius, Praeparatio Evangelica, ix. 28 f.) show him as a notable person, dressed up in Greek verses so as to appear inferior in no way (save in the quality of the verses themselves)

---

[1] R. Reitzenstein, Poimandres (Leipzig, 1904), p. 204, n. 1.

to Achilles and Agamemnon. But to introduce Moses into the field of Greek drama was perhaps a dangerous step. Artapan (second century B.C.) is by no means so innocent (Eusebius, *Praeparatio*, ix. 27). He equates the Hebrew name Moses with the Greek Musaeus, and quotes the view that Moses-Musaeus became the teacher of Orpheus, and bestowed many benefits upon men—not only religious but mechanical and nautical too. He assigned as gods to the several districts (*nomes*) of Egypt cats, dogs, and ibises.

> For this reason . . . Moses was beloved by the crowds (ὄχλοι), and by the priests was counted worthy of divine honour (ἰσοθέου τιμῆς), and called Hermes because of his interpretation (ἑρμηνεία) of the sacred writings.

Josephus's *Against Apion* shows from a different angle the recklessness with which legends about Moses were manufactured; there is no difficulty in thinking that some Jews, not too rigidly attached to the ancestral faith, indulged in similar fantasy with a view to answering slanders, and even going one better than the slanderers.

Some went further still, with the result that Moses finds a place in the magic that flourished in Egypt, as elsewhere. It will suffice to quote from a papyrus referred to by Reitzenstein (*op. cit.* pp. 184 f.):

> I call upon thee, the headless one, who createdst heaven and earth, who createdst night and day, who createdst light and darkness. Thou art Osoronnophris [the good Osiris], whom no one ever has seen, thou art Jabas [? *y-h-w-h*], thou art Japos. Thou didst distinguish right and wrong, thou didst make male and female, thou didst appoint (ἔδειξας) seed and fruits, thou didst make men to love and to hate one another. I am Moses thy prophet, to whom thou didst deliver thy perfected mysteries for Istrael. . . . Hear me; I am messenger (ἄγγελος) of (*phapro*) Osoronnophris; this is my true name which is given to the prophets of Istrael. . . . Hear me, and drive out this demon. . . . Headless one, relieve N.N. of the demon that oppresses him. . . . This is the Lord of gods, this is the Lord of the world, this is he whom the winds

fear. . . . I am the headless demon, who have sight in my feet, the mighty one, the immortal fire. I am the truth, he who hates that wrongs should happen in the cosmos. . . . I am the grace of the age (ἡ χάρις τοῦ αἰῶνος). . . .

It would be a mistake to treat all this nonsense as if it were a 'theology', in which Moses became a semi-divine, or demonic, being, acting, Hermes-like, as a messenger and prophet who could be indifferently described as Osiris and the God of Israel. It was the custom of magicians and exorcists to heap together as many impressive names as they could think of without much regard to their meaning and relevance. Yet even so the papyrus shows the sort of status that could be popularly accorded to Moses at least on the fringe of Judaism. Some might speak of Thoth, some of Hermes; others would speak of Moses. It was a matter mainly of linguistic environment; and one need not doubt that, in the border-country between Judaism and heathenism, very unbiblical things were often said about Moses.

The material I have briefly sketched represents in fact a simple and, given a certain environment, inevitable development. Moses was the central figure in Jewish religion; they were his writings that were read week by week in the synagogue, and the sacrificial worship carried out at the headquarters of the people was based on his enactment. The many peculiar customs that marked the Jews off from their neighbours were traced back to him. Even more important, Moses was the central figure in the drama of redemption, upon which the national, religious, and liturgical life of the people rested. True, the Old Testament constantly insisted that it was God himself, no other, who wrought deliverance for Israel; but, in an age and an environment accustomed to look for secondary figures as mediators both of knowledge and of salvation, Moses was an inevitable Jewish choice. A Jew such as Philo with his solid faithfulness to the revealed religion of Scripture could use this sort of language as at most an illustration, but there were others, as we have seen, who were less securely founded, and for them it was easy to assimilate Moses to the non-Jewish religious presuppositions which they had absorbed from their neighbours.

How far did this tendency affect Palestinian Judaism? Probably much more than has often been recognized. It has recently been suggested[1] that the Passover Haggadah contains a legend ascribing the birth of Moses to a supernatural cause. It was not in the strict sense a *virgin* birth, because Aaron and Miriam had already been born to Moses' mother; yet his birth took place because God 'knew' her. The evidence falls short of proof, but it is worth noting, and it accords with the belief that when Moses was born the house was filled with (supernatural) light.[2] There is some evidence for a corresponding belief about the death of Moses. According to Baba Bathra, 17a (a baraita),[3] there were six over whom the angel of death had no power: Abraham, Isaac, Jacob, Moses, Aaron, and Miriam. This is proved, as far as Moses is concerned, by the use in Deut. xxxiv. 5 of the phrase '*al-pī γ-h-w-h*; literally, at the mouth of the Lord. This was taken to mean that Moses' death was the result of God's kiss. The same passage (Baba Bathra 17a) adds that the body of Moses did not suffer corruption. It would be wrong to pay much attention to these assertions, still more to the late belief that Moses appeared on earth after his death.[4] To be taken more seriously is the description of Moses as 'the first redeemer', in the numerous analogies drawn between him and 'the latter redeemer', that is, the Messiah. The fact that orthodox Judaism seems to have made no use of the prophecy in Deut. xviii. 15 of a prophet 'like unto me' may well be due to the fact that Christians (though not Paul; possibly in view of what follows we should substitute for 'Christians', 'Samaritans and sectaries') had appropriated the verse. The Samaritans used the prophecy in a messianic sense; the Qumran sectaries apparently did so too.[5] Certainly they venerated Moses, and in

[1] D. Daube, *The New Testament and Rabbinic Judaism* (London, 1956), pp. 5-9.
[2] Evidence in S.B. i, p. 78; ii, p. 678.
[3] Quoted in S.B. i, p. 755.                    [4] See S.B. i, p. 755.
[5] *The Manual of Discipline*, ix. 11 is not conclusive evidence for this, as K. G. Kuhn suggests (*New Testament Studies*, i (1955), p. 178;) but Deut. xviii. 18 f. now appears in the Qumran *Testimonia*.

this at least they were at one with orthodox Judaism. Judaism was more and more becoming aware of itself as a religion of salvation, and in its religious development the legendary Moses figure as well as the historical Moses played an important part.

In view of the material we have now briefly surveyed Paul's treatment of Moses seems strikingly temperate. For him Moses is no quasi-divine figure. Nor does he think of Christ as a new Moses, a 'latter redeemer' conceived on the model of the former. The only phrase that could suggest this is 'baptism into Moses' (I Cor. x. 2), and there, as we have seen, the reverse is the truth. Paul works back from Christ to Moses, understanding Moses in the light of Christ, not Christ in the light of Moses. What then is the role of Moses in Paul's unfolding of the divine purpose?

We must return to Gal. iii at the point where our earlier study of the chapter broke off. God made promises to Abraham and to his seed. For Abraham himself, in that he had faith, the promises were in some measure fulfilled; but he received them only in faith, and complete fulfilment awaited the coming of the 'seed', equated by Paul with Christ. Upon this scene came Moses and the law, with no more power to upset the covenant of promise than any third party has to invalidate or alter a will. The covenant (or testament—διαθήκη) with Abraham had been made by God himself (Gal. iii. 17), and therefore nothing could annul it, so as to make the promise of no effect. Whatever the law may do, it does not abrogate the promise. Further, it is clear that the new principle of law does not supplant the old principle of promise as the basis of the inheritance promised to Abraham and his seed. Law and promise are mutually exclusive terms (Rom. iv. 14).

The law belonged strictly to the interim period[1] between the time when it was given and the coming of the seed (ἄχρις ἂν ἔλθῃ τὸ σπέρμα, Gal. iii. 19). A promise also is an interim arrangement, for a promise lapses as soon as it is fulfilled; the interimistic character of the law is thus not a disparagement of it. When the seed comes, both promise and law cease, in their

---

[1] See below, p. 65.

old meaning. Law and promise, however, terminate in different ways, and the arrival of the seed who was to be both agent and recipient of the promise was the signal for the abrogation of the law. The law, moreover, was shown to be inferior to the promise by the way in which it was given. God himself made the promise to Abraham, speaking face to face, God to man. But the law was not given to a man but to a people; and it was given not by God himself but by the angels. It was for this reason that Moses was needed. Two groups, one of angels and one of men, cannot deal directly with each other; they need a go-between, a μεσίτης (Gal. iii. 19). This subordinate office Moses filled. There are few passages in Paul's writings more offensive to Jewish sentiment than this. Other Christians (Acts vii. 53; Heb. ii. 2) regarded the presence of the angels as throwing lustre upon the occasion—both upon the law that was given and upon the people who received it. This was the rabbinic attitude. A late but representative passage (Pesiqta Rabbathi 21) is quoted in S.B. iii, p. 554:

> Why did the angels come down at the giving of the law? R. Hiyya b. Rabba said, To do honour to the Torah. R. Hiyya b. Jose said, To do honour to Israel.

Most Jews would have agreed with both Rabbis, and seen nothing contradictory in their views. Paul's expression 'by the hand of a mediator' (ἐν χειρὶ μεσίτου) probably reflects a Hebrew expression 'al yᵉḏē sarsōr (at the hands of a mediator), and the position of Moses as sarsōr was undoubtedly understood as one of the most outstanding privilege and dignity. Moses was to the Rabbis no mere go-between; he was also mediator, in the sense of intercessor and advocate.[1]

In contrast with this, Moses takes for Paul the character of a

---

[1] For evidence see N. Johansson, *Parakletoi* (Lund, 1940). Thus 'in ancient Israel it was obviously Moses, "the man of God", who was thought of as the advocate beyond all others' (p. 5). It was not otherwise at a later time: 'That Moses was the advocate beyond all others in ancient Israel was strongly emphasised in late Judaism' (p. 67). 'Among men of God Moses naturally took first place. His character as advocate, intercessor, and mediator did not grow weaker as time went on, but stronger. References to Moses as advocate for the people of Israel are relatively more frequent in Midrash and Talmud than in the Old Testament' (p. 161).

postman, or telephone operator—an astounding reversal. But
there is more in the context. The law was added to the promise
(this in itself implies that the law was an extra, not a fundamental religious datum), 'on account of transgressions' (τῶν
παραβάσεων χάριν). This expression is not unambiguous, but
comparison with Rom. v (especially verse 20) and vii (*e.g.*
verse 9) makes its meaning clear. The law was added not to
hold sin in check, but to increase it, and especially in the form
of παράβασις (or παράπτωμα)—concrete, observable, assessable
transgression. Between Adam and Moses this kind of sin had
been impossible (Rom. v. 14); with Moses, the deficiency was
made up in good measure.

In verse 21, Paul halts, wondering if he has gone too far. He
has turned the whole of rabbinic theology upside down. Does
his argument imply that the law of Moses is contrary to the
promises spoken to Abraham? that the law was given not by
God but by the devil? Certainly not. Everything in the law is
right; men only need to do it in order to be righteous. Paul
returns in thought to the passage he had quoted in verse 12:
The man who has done the commandments shall live in them.[1]
But the law was not addressed to men who were in a position
freely and effectively to choose to be obedient. It was addressed
to a race which, ever since the time of Adam, had been under
sentence of death. And the one thing the law needed, in these
circumstances, to do, was the one thing it could not do. The
law offered life to those who could obey it; it did not offer life
to dead men in order that they might obey it. This weakness of
the law (cf. Rom. viii. 3) vitiated its existence; it could not do
what it professed to do, because its setting was wrong. It
belonged to this age, and thus came under the dominion of
flesh, sin, and death.

What then did the law achieve? It issued not (as Judaism
taught) in freedom, but in bondage: the Scripture shut up all
under sin (verse 22). Before faith came, we were kept under

---

[1] This suggests that the ambiguity of τῶν παραβάσεων χάριν may be
significant; in some circumstances the law might have held sin in check, but
in the circumstances in which it was given its effect was the reverse.

guard, locked up (verse 23). The law has been our παιδαγωγός
up to the time of Christ—not an instructor, but a slave who sees
that the boy committed to his care does not play truant but gets
safely to school. It resembles the guardians and stewards under
whose jurisdiction an heir must live—in conditions no better
than slavery—until he comes of age, and enjoys the right of
disposal of what all the time has been his own property.

The prison in which the law thus incarcerated mankind had
one exit only; this was the way of faith. The law did not, as it
were, educate man *up* to faith, or *up* to Christ, providing the
necessary elementary education before the higher reaches of
religious knowledge could be attained. Its effect was to demonstrate that there was only one way, the way of faith, all others
being barred in man's face. The law is the ultimate *reductio ad
absurdum* of all religion and ethics. If this system, which came
from God himself, could in this age lead only to condemnation
and death, no other could possibly be effective. The way
forward must be a way beyond religion, and beyond morals.

This is the more favourable of two ways of looking at the
law of Moses. The less favourable connects it with the elemental
astral spirits under whose control (destiny, εἱμαρμένη) life was
imprisoned. Thus Gal. iv. 3:

> So (οὕτως, like the heir not yet of age) we too (καὶ ἡμεῖς—
> not Gentiles only but Jews also; or how could Paul say 'we'?),
> when we were children, were enslaved under the elemental
> spirits (ὑπὸ τὰ στοιχεῖα τοῦ κόσμου).

This is the same bondage or imprisonment as that described in
the previous chapter. Paul returns to it in iv. 8 ff. Here he is
not speaking of himself but of the Gentile Christians in Galatia.
Previously, in their ignorance, they had been enslaved to no-
gods, idols—τοῖς φύσει μὴ οὖσιν θεοῖς. Their conversion meant
not that they discovered the truth about God but that God took
knowledge of them, delivering them from their bondage. They
are now proposing to be circumcised, to submit (as Paul insists)
to the whole law. To do this would, he says, be to return to the
feeble and poverty-stricken elements (τὰ ἀσθενῆ καὶ πτωχὰ

στοιχεῖα), and thus to resume the old position of bondage. The full force of this must be grasped. For Gentile Christians to Judaize is to return to heathenism—nothing less.

Certainly Paul was aware of the immense difference between Jewish and pagan religion. He knew that no other people could compete with his own in zeal for God, and in the enthusiastic, self-sacrificing pursuit of righteousness. But no less than other religions, Judaism belonged to the age that had been inaugurated through Adam's transgression, and was coming to an end in Christ. The effect of the law was to demonstrate beyond all doubt that those who lived under it belonged to a world which was under the authority of sin rather than the authority of God. It belonged to Adam's world; everything in this world, dominated by evil spirits, was liable to corruption, and *corruptio optimi pessima*. I may point out in passing—there is scarcely time to do more—that this observation throws a great deal of light on the problem of the law in Rom. vii, and especially on the contrast in the closing verses of that chapter between what appear to be *two* laws (verses 22 f.):

> I agree with the law of God as far as the inward man (ἔσω ἄνθρωπος) is concerned, but I see another law in my members, making war upon the law of my mind, and taking me prisoner by the law of sin which is in my members.

What Paul says here may be viewed from several angles, but it is surely true that there is one divine law, one truth about the meaning of man's existence *coram deo*; but that this one divine law is bound to appear in different lights and in different shapes as it is considered in the evil age which has fallen under the dominion of evil spirits, and in the age to come which has been inaugurated through the death and resurrection of Jesus.[1]

Here is the explanation of the connection Paul sees between the law and the elemental spirits (στοιχεῖα). It is not simply, as is sometimes said, that the calendrical aspect of the law shows

---

[1] What is involved here and in the following pages is the whole question of the relation between Law and Gospel. I believe that the solution of this venerable—and urgent—problem is to be sought on the lines indicated here; but this is not the place to work it out in detail.

it to be dependent on the movements of the heavenly bodies, though Paul uses this fact as an illustration of what he means (Gal. iv. 10). The truth is rather that the law as Judaism knew it belonged to the age in which the elements ruled through destiny. The thought of Gal. iii, iv is governed throughout by the idea of a *terminus ad quem*:

iii. 19: It was added on account of transgressions, *until* (ἄχρις ἄν) the seed should come.

iii. 23: *Before* (πρό) faith came we were kept under guard under the law, shut up *until* (εἰς) faith should be revealed.

iii. 24 f.: The law has been our tutor *up to* the time of (εἰς) Christ, that we might be justified by faith. *But now* that faith has come (ἐλθούσης δέ), we are *no longer* (οὐκέτι) under a tutor.

iv. 1 f.: *As long as* (ἐφ' ὅσον χρόνον) the heir is under age . . . *until* (ἄχρι) the time appointed by his father.

iv. 3. f.: *When* (ὅτε) we were under age . . . *but when* (ὅτε δέ) the fullness of the time came. . . .

The force of these temporal limits and contrasts cannot be missed. It is the new Christian eschatology that disposes of the law as it had been understood in Judaism. We note at the same time that faith, justification, and baptism (see iii. 27) are all of them eschatological events.

This observation will lead us back to I Cor. x, the passage which, as we have seen, gives us the most positive evaluation of Moses in the whole Pauline literature. Of the events that took place under Moses at the time of the Exodus Paul says:

These things happened to them as an object-lesson (τυπικῶς), and they were written down for our admonition, who find ourselves overtaken by the end of the age (x. 11).

The law of Moses, and the events connected with it, gain their typical significance from the fact that the context in which the law was delivered was that of the deliverance of the people from bondage by God. This in itself served as a prefigurement of what God was to do at the end of the age, when a new people would be delivered out of the evil age in which their existence was set (Gal. i. 4). This correspondence gives Paul his immediate point: No more than the Israelites at the time of the

Exodus will the Corinthian Christians be automatically pre-
served by their sacraments from sin and punishment. But it goes
further than this. It is because of the correspondence between
the circumstances of the Exodus and those of the Church that
the law of Moses bears witness to the Gospel as other religious
and legal systems do not. In Christ, the righteousness of God
has been manifested apart from law, yet at the same time
attested by the law (Rom. iii. 21). This sentence only crystallizes
what is scattered all over the Pauline corpus. It is not merely
that the law is good *as law*; it also bears witness to that which
is not law at all.[1] It is very important that Paul quotes the
Pentateuch in order to indicate what he means by both the
'righteousness of the law' and the 'righteousness of faith'.

Rom. x. 5: Moses writes of the righteousness of the law,
that the man who has done it shall live by it.

x. 6 ff.: The righteousness of faith speaks thus: Say not in
your heart, Who shall ascend into heaven? that is, to bring
Christ down; or, Who shall descend into the abyss? that is,
to bring Christ up from the dead. But what does it say? The
word is near you, in your mouth and in your heart—that is,
the word of faith which we preach.

One passage is from Leviticus, the other from Deuteronomy;
both from the Torah. We may compare the discussion of true
and false Judaism, true and false circumcision, in Rom. ii,
where the point is the same. Rightly understood in the context
of the gracious, delivering action of God, the law bears witness
to the Gospel, and commands precisely that relation with God
in which Abraham reversed the sin of Adam. The witness
lapses, however, as soon as the law is removed to a different
context.

The relation between the law and the Gospel can also be
taken, as it were, in reverse. Christ, says Paul (Rom. x. 4), is
the end of the law with a view to effecting righteousness for
everyone who believes ($\tau\acute{\epsilon}\lambda o\varsigma$ $\nu\acute{o}\mu o\upsilon$ $X\rho\iota\sigma\tau\grave{o}\varsigma$ $\epsilon\grave{\iota}\varsigma$ $\delta\iota\kappa\alpha\iota o\sigma\acute{\upsilon}\nu\eta\nu$
$\pi\alpha\nu\tau\grave{\iota}$ $\tau\hat{\omega}$ $\pi\iota\sigma\tau\epsilon\acute{\upsilon}o\nu\tau\iota$). This recalls the notes and limitations of

---

[1] In the ordinary sense of the word law (or *lex*, or $\nu\acute{o}\mu o\varsigma$); the Hebrew *tōrāh*
has different overtones.

time that we noticed above in Gal. iii, iv. Christ is the end of the law because with him came the new age, whereas the law belonged to the old age. Righteousness is now realized by a new divine gift, accepted in faith; but this does not mean that the law as such is wrong, or that it is a misleading account of what God requires from men, or of his relations with men. Otherwise Paul could not speak as he does of the law of Christ:

Gal. vi. 2: Bear one another's burdens, and so you will fulfil the law of Christ.

I Cor. ix. 21: To those without law I became as one without law (though I am not outside God's law (ἄνομος θεοῦ) but within Christ's law (ἔννομος Χριστοῦ)), in order that I might gain those who are without law.

Further, we must recall Rom. xiii. 8 ff., where Paul sums up the Old Testament law in the command of love, which he certainly regards as binding upon Christians. By means of this precept, and for their own good, God continues to command his creatures to live in a way consistent with the order of their creation, that is, to recognize their universal obligation to himself, and their inter-relatedness with one another. This obligation and this inter-relatedness now for the first time are realized —in the person of Jesus Christ; and they are vindicated by God in the resurrection of his crucified Son. This observation, however, is leading us on to material that must be deferred to the fourth and fifth chapters. What we must for the present notice is simply the correspondence between the Mosaic dispensation and the Christian, and the difference between them.

There is thus after all a kinship between Abraham and Moses. Each represents (Paul was no Marcionite) the true relationship with God for which man was created, but each suffers under the same radical disability; both belong exclusively within the age of the demonic forces of destiny (the στοιχεῖα), or, to put it differently, of the flesh (σάρξ; cf. Rom. viii. 3). Neither of them experiences the victory over the powers of evil, which did not take place until, with the fullness of time, God sent forth his Son.

# IV

# CHRIST

No attempt can be made in the short space of this chapter to
treat Paul's Christological thought as a whole. In this compass
Christology can be treated, if at all, only from the special point
of view that is determined by the general pattern of this book.
There is practically no limit to the ideas current in first-century
Judaism regarding the figure of the Messiah—at least, he would
be a rash man who claimed to be able to list them all ; yet it can
probably be agreed that most (not all) Jews of the period were
at one in the conviction that, as great men such as Abraham,
Moses, and here we must add David, had emerged at decisive
points in their past history, so the future also would be shaped
by another decisive figure, another anointed of the Lord, the
Anointed One *par excellence*. It is reasonably safe to add that all
varieties of messianic thought in Judaism had in common the
hope and belief that in his Messiah God would do some new
thing; but this by no means precluded the view that the
Messiah would be recognizably one, even though the last and
greatest, in a series. And this in turn raises the question how
the Messiah and his work are related, positively and negatively,
to his predecessors and their work.

To look at this from another angle: we have in each of the
preceding chapters noted that some sort of connection exists
between their subjects—Adam, Abraham, and Moses—and the
Christ. Adam is described as a figure of the Coming One
(Rom. v. 14).  Abraham, who put his trust in God's power to
raise the dead and call into being that which does not exist, pre-
figures the Christian believer, who believes in God who raised
Christ from the dead; Christ himself is Abraham's seed (Rom.
iv. 17, 24; Gal. iii. 16). Moses and the men of his generation

CHRIST 69

serve as examples for the instruction of Christian believers
(I Cor. x. 6, 11), and Moses's law bears witness to the Gospel
(Rom. iii. 21). Our present task must be first to see what
Christological use Paul makes of the figures of Adam, Abraham,
and Moses, and then to inquire what theological questions are
raised for us by the process.

We begin with Adam. In every passage in which Adam is
named, there is specific reference to Christ. The relevant texts
must be recalled.

Rom. v. 14: Who [Adam] is a figure ($\tau\acute{\upsilon}\pi os$) of the Coming
One ($\tau o\hat{\upsilon}$ $\mu\acute{\epsilon}\lambda\lambda o\nu\tau os$).

The chapter continues with a running comparison and contrast
between Adam and Christ: by his transgression, Adam brought
upon the race sin, condemnation, and death; Christ brought
grace, justification, and life.

I Cor. xv. 21 f.: Since by man ($\delta\iota'$ $\acute{\alpha}\nu\theta\rho\acute{\omega}\pi o\upsilon$) came death,
by man ($\delta\iota'$ $\acute{\alpha}\nu\theta\rho\acute{\omega}\pi o\upsilon$) also came the resurrection of the
dead. For as in Adam ($\acute{\epsilon}\nu$ $\tau\hat{\omega}$ 'A$\delta\acute{\alpha}\mu$) all die, so also in Christ
($\acute{\epsilon}\nu$ $\tau\hat{\omega}$ X$\rho\iota\sigma\tau\hat{\omega}$) shall all be made alive.

xv. 45-9: It is written: The first man Adam became a
living soul ($\psi\upsilon\chi\acute{\eta}\nu$); the last Adam became a life-giving
spirit ($\pi\nu\epsilon\hat{\upsilon}\mu\alpha$). Only it is not the spiritual ($\pi\nu\epsilon\upsilon\mu\alpha\tau\iota\kappa\acute{o}\nu$)
that comes first, but the natural ($\psi\upsilon\chi\iota\kappa\acute{o}\nu$), then the spiritual.
The first man comes out of the earth, made of dust; the
second man comes from heaven. As is the man made of dust,
so are those who are made of dust; and as is the heavenly
Man, so are the heavenly men. And as we have borne the
image of the man made of dust, so we shall bear also the
image of the heavenly Man.

To these should be added Phil. ii. 5-11, which will be brought
into the ensuing discussion, though the name of Adam is not
mentioned in it. Some of this material has already been considered;[1] here two special points call for notice.

(1) Adam and Christ are said to have been responsible for
analogous acts; that is, in analogous circumstance, the one

[1] See pp. 14-17.

made the wrong, the other the right choice. One was obedient, the other disobedient. This is the theme of Rom. v. 12-21 (and perhaps—see below—of Phil. ii. 5-11 also). But a question immediately suggests itself: Can these two really be said to have been in analogous circumstances? The position of Adam is reasonably clear, and has already been discussed. He was placed in favourable surroundings, where all he was required to do was to live as the creature that he was; to live, that is, in humble dependence on his Maker, and in the exercise of the sovereignty over all other created beings which had been committed to him. Instead of doing this, he decided to seek independence for himself, and to deal with God on terms of equality. We have seen that the consequences of this decision were not only his own loss of the privileges given in his creation, but also the bringing of the world as a whole under the sway of evil powers. So much for Adam. Was Christ ever in a position truly analogous to this? According to Phil. ii. 6 he did not count equality with God a ἁρπαγμός. If we take this word to mean (as it may well do) *res rapienda*, a prize to be snatched at, we may see in it a picture of what Adam did; it was in snatching at equality with God that he fell from the high (but not divine) position that had been allotted to him. But Paul is speaking of Christ; is it in this case reasonable to translate ἁρπαγμός as *res rapienda*? Must we not take it to denote *res rapta*, something already possessed which Christ was graciously willing to surrender for the good of mankind? There is a probable solution of this problem, though there is no space here to work it out in detail. Since the work of Lohmeyer[1] it has been widely recognized that in Phil. ii we have a pre-Pauline hymn, quoted by Paul at this point because it served his purpose of inculcating selflessness by the example of Christ—and perhaps also because he knew that the Philippians would recognize it and acknowledge its truth. This suggestion I take to be essentially true. We must not, however, assume that Paul quoted the hymn in

[1] E. Lohmeyer, 'Kyrios Jesus. Eine Untersuchung zu Phil. 2. 5-11', in *Sitzungsberichte der Heidelberger Akademie der Wissenschaften*, phil.-hist. Kl. 1927/28 (4). See also the discussion and bibliography in F. W. Beare, *The Epistle to the Philippians* (London, 1959), pp. 40 ff., 73-88.

its original form and without modification. I may here recall the pre-Pauline formula quoted by Paul at Rom. i. 3 f., but not quoted by him in its original form. I have argued elsewhere[1] that the naïve adoptionism of 'who was appointed Son of God, according to the Holy Spirit, after the resurrection from the dead' was incompatible with Paul's own belief in the incarnation of a pre-existent Son of God; hence Paul's addition of 'in power' (ἐν δυνάμει). At the resurrection Christ came to be the Son of God *in power*, whereas previously (during the ministry) he had been the Son of God in weakness. It is a plausible suggestion that in Phil. ii Paul may have similarly edited the material that he used. Whether he made use of the grammatical ambiguity of ἁρπαγμός we need not discuss (though this is a question that would have to be discussed in a full treatment of the subject); the matter was adequately dealt with by the insertion of 'being in the form of God' (ἐν μορφῇ θεοῦ ὑπάρχων). The word μορφή was probably chosen as suggesting creation in the image of God without pressing the analogy with Adam too hard; it also implied more than this.[2] The resulting picture loses clarity of outline, and this accounts for the difficulty that expositors have always found in it. It would be a simple clear-cut picture if we could say: Christ, like Adam, was a man; unlike Adam, he was an obedient man, and did not clutch at that which was above him. Because of his obedience and humility God rewarded him with the lordship over all creation which Adam was created for, but lost. This is clear. It may be what the pre-Pauline hymn said. But it was not true; Paul could not accept its implications because they were inconsistent with his Son-of-God Christology. He was perhaps the first, though certainly not the last, theologian to encounter the paradox of the person of one who is confessed as both truly human and truly divine. We may recall the fact that in Rom. v we meet not only the expected *parallels* between Adam and Christ (*e.g.*, 'As through one act of transgression

---

[1] See *Romans*, pp. 18-21.
[2] Though scarcely so much as Lightfoot claimed, in his well-known note. In addition to the commentaries, see also J. Behm, in *T.W.N.T.* iv, pp. 758 ff.

condemnation resulted for all men, *so* through one act of righteousness justification, issuing in life, resulted for all men', v. 18), but also the surprising contrasts (*e.g.*, 'The act of grace was *not* like the act of sin', v. 15). The act of Jesus was the act of an obedient man, but at the same time it was the act of a gracious God.[1] It was, however, truly both: this is essential to Paul's thought about Christ and about redemption. Thus (to return to Phil. ii. 6) Paul, seeing more clearly than his predecessors, affirms that for Christ equality with God was both *res rapta* and *res rapienda*. As the eternal Son of God, he had it; yet emptied himself and became obedient (cf. II Cor. viii. 9). As Man, the new Adam, he had it not; yet did not snatch at it, but chose rather the life of obedient and dependent creatureliness for which God made him. Certainly there is confusion here; but it arises directly out of redemption as Paul understood it, in its anthropological and cosmic (or mythical) aspects.[2] In Christ the defective anthropological situation was rectified because at last an obedient and believing man was found; and the cosmic situation was retrieved, because the Son of God was humble enough to enter the world, which, though it was God's creation, had now fallen under the dominion of the demonic powers.

(2) The second point is one that must be handled relatively briefly at this stage, since it is a major theme of the fifth chapter. It is made clear in the passages under review that neither Adam nor Christ acted as an individual.

> As through the disobedience of the one man the mass of men (οἱ πολλοί) were constituted sinners, so also through the obedience of the one man the mass of men shall be constituted righteous (Rom. v. 19).
> As in Adam all die, so also in Christ shall all be made alive (I Cor. xv. 22).

The question raised here is crystallized in the meaning of the word *in* (ἐν) in the second quotation. In what sense is the whole race *in* Adam? Is it in the same sense or in some other

---

[1] See *Romans*, pp. 113 ff.          [1] See pp. 20 f.

that all men are *in* Christ? Are the 'all' who are in Christ the same as the 'all' who are in Adam? That is, is the effect of redemption co-extensive with the reign of sin and death, and thus universal? All we need do at this point is recall the conclusion reached at the end of the preceding paragraph. A distinction must be made between the anthropological and the cosmic effects of Adam's work, and of Christ's. As far as Adam is concerned, both are necessarily universal; Christ's victory over the demonic powers must also be universal, but the same cannot be said of his anthropological achievement. If the powers are defeated, they are defeated, and this will be true for all mankind; but it will not necessarily follow from this that each several man is rightly related to God. Moreover, Paul's understanding of both these themes can be grasped only if we are prepared to view them in the eschatological framework in which he has placed them. This we are not yet ready to do; it suggests, however, our next task, which is to consider the remaining Adam passage, I Cor. xv. 45-9.

The passage is quoted above (p. 69). The context will be recalled. At the beginning of the paragraph (verse 35), Paul puts the question, How are the dead raised? With what kind of body do they come? Doubtless the question had been put to him, and by Greeks, incredulous at the notion of the 'standing up of corpses' (ἀνάστασις νεκρῶν). It is an unintelligent question. The inquirer has misunderstood the meaning of *body* (σῶμα). Paul is perhaps hard on his Greek reader, who could scarcely be expected to understand σῶμα otherwise than materially. Paul's own understanding of the word was much more flexible. There are (he argues) different kinds of σῶμα, adapted by God to various purposes. He drifts perhaps a little from the main theme when he proceeds to illustrate the different kinds of flesh and degrees of glory that God has made, but he comes back to it sharply in verse 42: So also is the resurrection of the dead. A seed is sown in the ground; something assuredly comes up, only it is not the seed, but a plant. Similarly, when a dead body is sown in the ground, *something* will assuredly arise; yet not precisely the body that was buried. In view of natural processes, why should we not readily accept God's power to produce a new and appropriate kind of body? Paul sums up the difference between the old body and the new by describing the former as ψυχικόν, the latter as πνευματικόν. There should be no more difficulty in accepting the existence of a πνευματικὸν σῶμα than in accepting that of the σώματα ψυχικά with which we are familiar. This position Paul proceeds to develop (οὕτως καί) by means of the description of Adam in Gen. ii. He quotes Gen. ii. 7 with two explanatory additions. He adds πρῶτος (first) in view of the ἔσχατος (last) that is to come, and 'Αδάμ (Adam) as an emphatic reference to the Hebrew, which is not adequately represented by the Greek ἄνθρωπος (man). The immediate point of the quotation, though not expressed in so many words, is that the Man, the Adam, of the Genesis story was such a σῶμα ψυχικόν as Paul has spoken of—a being of determinate form animated by a ψυχή. But this is not all. Since Paul has demonstrated the existence of more than one kind of σῶμα, he feels free to conclude that when Gen. ii states the existence of one kind, it implies also the existence of another, that of the last Adam, and he goes on to supplement the quotation accordingly. The last Adam also was a body—Paul did not think of disembodied existence—only that which animated his body was not ψυχή but πνεῦμα, and it is characteristic of πνεῦμα in biblical thought that it not only is alive but gives life; as Paul says, it is ζωοποιοῦν (cf. John vi. 63). This, at least, is the way Paul's argument runs; it will be observed that his thought moves too rapidly for him actually to state that the last Adam was a σῶμα πνευματικόν, though this is implied by the context; what he says is that the last Adam became a life-giving spirit. The form of this expression is suggested by the wording of Gen. ii. 7 (I Cor. xv. 45). Here, in a different form, we meet a paradox that we have seen before. The new, last, Adam is 'ā̱dām, ἄνθρωπος, MAN, just as his predecessor was; but at the same time he is what his predecessor was not—namely, πνεῦμα. The exact bearing of verse 46 is not immediately clear. It will be noted, first, that Paul emphasizes the temporal sequence of natural and spiritual,

and, secondly, that he uses the two adjectives, ψυχικόν and
πνευματικόν, not in the masculine gender, as if they simply
referred to two men, but in the neuter. The latter fact shows
that he is still thinking of bodies, σώματα, by which we may
reasonably understand orders of human existence. The former
fact shows that Paul sees the two orders of human existence as
eschatologically, not ontologically, determined and related. His
point becomes clearer if we compare it with Philo's exegesis of
Gen. i, ii—not that Paul is likely to have read Philo, or referred
to him specifically, though it is not impossible that Philo's
exegesis of Genesis had spread beyond his own circle in
Alexandria. According to Philo, Gen. i and ii describe the
creation of two distinct 'men'. The one created in Gen. i in the
image of God is archetypal man, a Platonic ideal man; he who
is described in Gen. ii. 7 as formed of the dust of the earth is
empirical man, fashioned according to the archetype, but com-
pounded of matter and spirit. Inevitably, the 'spiritual' man[1]
came first; the 'natural' man followed. This view of humanity
Paul rejects, preferring eschatology to Platonism.[2] His use of
πνευματικός and ψυχικός does not imply the contemporaneous
existence of higher and lower orders of humanity; the adjectives
denote the kinds of body, of existence, suitable to this age and
to the age to come. Christ, as the last Adam and life-giving
Spirit, is the inaugurator of the new age.

To eschatology Paul comes explicitly in I Cor. xv. 47, jump-
ing to a new contrast, as he had jumped in verse 45 from ψυχή
to πνεῦμα. In Gen. ii. 7 he read not only the word 'soul' (ψυχή)
but also 'dust' (χοῦς). This (if the idea of a second man be
granted at all) suggests as its counterpart 'heavenly' (ἐπου-
ράνιος). The first man was 'out of the earth' (ἐκ γῆς); the
second is 'out of heaven' (ἐξ οὐρανοῦ). But a man appearing
from heaven is a well-known Old Testament figure, the one
like a Son of man who appears with the clouds of heaven in

---

[1] ὁ κατὰ τὴν εἰκόνα, de Opificio Mundi, 134.
[2] This epigram must not be taken too far. See my article on 'New Testament Eschatology', in Scottish Journal of Theology, vi (1953), especially
p. 139; also T. F. Glasson, Greek Influence in Jewish Eschatology (London,
1961).

Dan. vii. Paul is too idiomatic in the use of Greek to employ
such a barbarism as ὁ υἱὸς τοῦ ἀνθρώπου (which is no more
Greek than 'the son of man' is English), but he is not independent either of the Jewish use of this term, or of the
Christian tradition that Jesus had used it to describe himself. If
further evidence is needed it may be found by turning back
to verses 23-8, where Paul uses both Ps. cx, the Psalm of the
Lord who sits at God's right hand with all his foes subjected
to him, and Ps. viii, the Psalm of the Son of man, to whom
God subjects the whole of creation. Jesus the heavenly Man is
he in whom man's rightful position in and over creation is
restored. But not yet; for he is still to come from heaven (Phil.
iii. 20 f.) to transform the 'body of our humiliation' (τὸ σῶμα
τῆς ταπεινώσεως ἡμῶν, i.e. the σῶμα ψυχικόν), to make it like
the 'body of his glory' (τὸ σῶμα τῆς δόξης αὐτοῦ, i.e. the
σῶμα πνευματικόν). This means (to return to the language of
I Cor. xv) that we who have borne the image of the earthy
Man shall bear[1] the image of the heavenly Man, when at
the resurrection we share with him the life of the age to
come.

Paul's picture of the second Man needs to be pieced together,
but it is coherent. What we have not learnt about it in the
present context is why the Man from heaven should first
appear on earth in the image of the earthy Man to suffer and
die. This is closely connected with the question, which must
be deferred for consideration in the next chapter, of the relation
between Jesus Christ and humanity as a whole.

We turn from Adam to Abraham. Here the relation involved is one not of type or figure, but of ancestry. Jesus Christ
is the seed (σπέρμα) of Abraham (Gal. iii. 16). God's promise
was addressed not only to Abraham but to his seed. Since
Abraham has long since gone to his rest, it will be for and
through the seed that the promise is fulfilled.

It is certainly true that in Genesis the promises are not
thought of as focused upon one person, but upon a long line of

---

[1] Reading the future indicative, φορέσομεν, not the aorist subjunctive, which
wrongly turns the passage into an exhortation.

descent, involving in each generation a plurality of persons. The Hebrew *zera'*, and the Greek σπέρμα, both translated 'seed', are both collective terms. Because of this, it is often said that in Gal. iii. 16 Paul is indulging in a piece of meaningless word-play quite incapable of sustaining an argument. The dative plural σπέρμασιν ('to seeds') is indeed practically unthinkable as Greek; but it does not follow that Paul is writing nonsense. The Old Testament narratives themselves make descent from Abraham a matter of rigorous predestination, a fact that Paul underlines in Rom. ix. For example, Ishmael was, humanly speaking, Abraham's seed; but the Old Testament is clear that it is in the line of Isaac, not of Ishmael, that Abraham's seed is counted. Similarly in the next generation: of the twins, Jacob and Esau, one was loved and the other hated. In that generation too the collective 'seed' was narrowed to one person. It is quite consistent with this approach that Paul should think of the 'seed' of Abraham as eventually concentrated in the one person, Jesus Christ.

The matter might also be looked at from the other end. It must not be assumed that the word Christ (Χριστός; used by Paul in Gal. iii. 16) is narrowly individual, and in no sense collective. In the Old Testament it is occasionally used in the plural;[1] moreover, the anointed king or priest was anointed precisely in order to represent his people. In the New Testament the word Christ is not used in the plural;[2] yet if Christ is one, there are many in Christ. The main point, however, is the plain assertion of Rom. ix. 7: 'seed' is not to be understood in terms of physical descent but of divine election. Now, quite independently of any word-play about σπέρμα, it is Paul's teaching that election, predestination, is effected by God in Jesus Christ, and never apart from him; and it is in Jesus Christ that the whole body of Christians are what they are, as the context in Gal. iii brings out. It is in him that they are sons of God (iii. 26); it is in him that Jew and Greek, slave and free,

---

[1] I Chron. xvi. 22; Ps. civ (cv). 15; Hab. iii. 13, though not in all MSS.
[2] Cf., however, I John ii. 20, 27, where it is said that all Christians have a χρῖσμα, or anointing.

male and female, become one person (εἷς ἐστε ἐν Χριστῷ Ἰησοῦ, iii. 28). Paul is in fact well aware that the word σπέρμα is a collective noun, but it denotes a collectivity that comes into existence only through God and in Jesus Christ. The last verse of the chapter sums the matter up:

> If you belong to Christ, then you are Abraham's seed (σπέρμα), heirs in terms of the promise (iii. 29).

'Descent', if you may call it that, from Abraham is a matter of election, and it passes through Christ as through a channel, in whom all that the person of Abraham adumbrated was fulfilled. The old collectivity of race had to be destroyed in order that the new collectivity might be established in Christ. Abraham as an Old Testament figure represents on the human side the primacy of faith—of obedient trust, of believing obedience. He also represents, on the divine side, God's intention to create a people for himself, and to do so on the basis of his own gracious and merciful power alone, for he uses as the fount of his family not a young and healthy human pair but an old man and an old woman, long past the begetting and bearing of children. Thus he shows himself to be the God who calls non-being into being, and brings life out of death, and is worthy of the trust Abraham places in him. He also shows himself to be free, for he is never tied to the process of heredity, but in each generation acts in electing grace.

The story of Israel after the flesh is made up of a series of approximations to this twofold pattern. On the human side, along with much unbelief and disobedience, there is also the record of a remnant, and of prophets who by word and deed recall the people to the rock whence they were hewn: 'Look unto Abraham your father' (Isa. li. 2). On the other side, the story turns again and again upon acts of divine deliverance, manifestations of grace and power which were more or less clearly understood to recall the gracious and creative work of divine election in Abraham. This twofold conviction may properly be described as the central core of Israelite religion in view of the thanksgiving and profession made by the individual Israelite at Firstfruits and also in the Passover Haggadah. In this declaration Jacob takes the place of his grandfather, but the sense is unchanged.

> I profess unto the Lord thy God that I am come unto the land which the Lord sware unto our fathers to give us. . . . A Syrian ready to perish was my father, and he went down into Egypt, and sojourned there, few in number: and he became there a nation, great, mighty, and populous: and the Egyptian evil entreated us, and afflicted us, and laid upon us hard bondage: and we cried unto the Lord, the God of our fathers, and the Lord heard our voice, and saw our afflictions, and our toil, and our oppression; and the Lord brought us forth out of Egypt with a mighty hand, and with an outstretched arm, and with great terribleness, and with signs, and with wonders (Deut. xxvi. 3-8).

This sense of electing and delivering grace, and of the thankfulness and trust with which man was bound to respond to it, was always at the heart of Jewish religion at its best. Yet, in the story of empirical Israel, obedience and faith are never more than approximated, and are often denied, and the acts of deliverance are all relative acts. It is only, according to the New Testament conviction, in Jesus Christ that obedience and faith came to perfect expression, and that at the same time the act of cosmic and universal deliverance took place. Jesus Christ is thus the *one* seed of Abraham, because nowhere else does the promise of blessing through perfect faith and consummated deliverance find realization. He is the heir who inherits the promise; but since the promise also includes the clause that 'in thy seed shall all the Gentiles be blessed', the enjoyment of the inheritance is not for Jesus Christ only, but for all, Jew and Gentile alike, who belong to him.

What has to be said here about Moses must be closely integrated into the foregoing. There are parts of the New Testament which suggest that Jesus was a new Moses. Paul does not take this view. It would be nearer the truth (though it would not exactly be the truth) to say that for him Moses and Christ stand over against each other as adversaries. So far as Moses represents the way of man's own religious and moral righteousness, he is the enemy. As we have seen, however, to look at Moses in this way is to misunderstand him, though, according to Paul, the misunderstanding was one of which Judaism itself was guilty. Moses himself preaches the righteousness of faith, though admittedly in such a way as to invite misunderstanding. When he is read, the veil lies on men's hearts.

The right way to understand Moses is to see him as (*a*) providing in the law a channel for the obedience of faith to flow in, and (*b*) supplying an outstanding example of the gracious, redeeming activity of God. The law is not contrary to the promises of God (Gal. iii. 21), but lays down the divine requirement of love (Rom. xiii. 8 ff.), which is not denied but confirmed in the Gospel. But love (ἀγάπη) is easily perverted into desire (ἐπιθυμία), and it was through this perversion that sin laid hands upon the law, and used it as its point of entry into human life (Rom. vii. 13). The 'law of Christ' (Gal. vi. 2) is not a new law, for it is the law of love which was already laid down by Moses, though laid down by him in such a way as to be readily capable of perversion. Christ therefore is not a new lawgiver, but the interpreter, or indeed the vindicator or establisher, of the old law (Rom. iii. 31). His interpretation of the law, however, is so radical, and so personal, that he becomes its end, and Moses fails to provide Paul with any positive Christological material; he remains fundamentally a contrasting figure.

It is now time to look back at the ground we have covered, and to consider what we have learnt regarding Paul's understanding of Jesus Christ. I take as starting-point the interesting and suggestive book by J. L. Leuba, *L'Institution et L'Événement* (Neuchâtel and Paris, 1950), and may be allowed first of all to recall the contrast worked out by Dr. Leuba, in relation to Christology and also to certain other themes. Some of the Christological terms used in the gospels are, he says, institutional; that is, they describe offices which Jesus when he came occupied and fulfilled. The clearest example is the term Messiah, with related expressions such as Son of David. The latter is the easiest of all to deal with; of any given man it may be affirmed that he was or was not descended from David; it is known in advance what the category 'Son of David' means, and it only needs to be stated that X or Y is or is not a person who fulfils the requirements. The term Messiah is not quite so clear because it is of wider scope and is not so easily defined; it is certain that the word suggested different ideas to different persons. Even so, however, it can be granted in advance that there is such an office as Messiahship, and it can then be simply affirmed that X or Y does or does not fill that office. In fact, it was, as we know, asserted that Jesus of Nazareth was descended from David, and was the Messiah. There is, however, another set of terms less easy to delimit. Dr. Leuba calls them 'spiritual titles'. 'Son of man' is one such term, for though it points back to Dan. vii, and has some affinity with I Enoch, it cannot be claimed that 'Son of man' constituted a definite office, which Judaism understood and was waiting to have filled. Rather, Jesus appeared claiming to be the Son of man—or, better, making cryptic affirmations about a Son of man who appears sometimes to be himself, sometimes another person. Clearest of all in this class of 'spiritual titles', though not common in the earlier strata of the gospel tradition, is the word κύριος (lord). Jesus is the Lord; he confronts men as one who transcends every known category, and enters the framework of human life from an alien world. Such terms as 'Son of man' and 'Lord' are not institutional, but place the person and work of Jesus within the realm of pure event, of that which is completely outside man's reckoning and control, and simply confronts him in grace and judgement.

This is a valuable analysis of Christological terms, though it is one that can be pushed too far and treated too mechanically. If we apply it to Paul's Christological thinking there is no doubt where his emphasis lies. There is in Paul very little of what may be called 'institutional Christology'. For example, Paul is not greatly interested in Jesus as the Son of David, or even as the Messiah. The common use of the double name Jesus Christ proves *both* that Paul did accept from those who

were Christians before him that Jesus was the Messiah, *and* that
this fact meant so little to him that he could use 'Christ' as a
mere name. This is not quite the whole truth; Rom. ix. 5 shows
that he was aware of Messiahship as a Jewish institution. But
there is little in the epistles to this effect. It would not, however,
be correct to go to the other extreme and assert that in the
epistles Jesus Christ confronts us as pure, undreamed of event.
Paul does not make use of many ready-made terms to describe
the person and work of Christ, but he knows that these
exist.

Our work on Adam, Abraham, and Moses illustrates Paul's
thought on this point. Certainly, Jesus is one who comes as an
alien from another world. No one can constrain his coming—
climb into heaven and bring him down. At the appointed
moment God sends his Son; in him he manifests his righteousness apart from law, that is, without direct reference to or
dependence on the previous religious structure of Israel. Yet
this manifestation is attested by the law and the prophets. The
religion and literature of Judaism had borne witness to their
own incompleteness, and need of a complement; and the
Pentateuch no less than the prophets had at least sketched the
shape this complement must take. From Moses we learn how
the complementary figure must be related to religion, and from
Abraham how he must be related to the company of God's
people. In each we see a human pattern of trust and obedience
which cries aloud for implementation by the free action of the
power of God in fulfilment of his promise. In the figure of
Adam something even more fundamental appears, for here is
Man created as Lord over God's other creatures, but denying
his relation with God, losing his lordship, and himself becoming
subject to gods many and lords many; this defaulting Man
points from himself to Man in his restoration, and indeed to
Man the restorer, the conqueror of the powers of evil.

Thus, for Paul, though Jesus Christ is the divine intruder, his
intrusion follows a pattern that could in a sense, and in some
degree, have been predicted. This observation suggests two
theological questions, which must now be discussed.

/ The first is that of the relation in Paul's thought between redemption and creation. That such a relation exists is clear; what kind of relation is it? Is it such a relation that Paul can argue from creation to redemption? Was Christ himself so manifestly active in creation that the created world bears witness to him; and so active in redemption that a direct continuity can be traced between the one work and the other?

Before we can handle this question seriously we must look briefly at another notable Christological passage, Col. i. 15-20. There have been several recent studies of this passage, of which I name especially those by E. Käsemann,[1] and E. Schweizer.[2] Space does not permit me to follow in detail the literary analyses conducted by these scholars, though each makes critical observations that contribute to the theological understanding of the passage. They agree that the passage as a whole is not Pauline in origin,[3] but was worked over before being incorporated into the epistle. Not only was the original material of the section non-Pauline; in its earliest state it was non-Christian. Dr. Käsemann, for example, points out that of the 112 words in Col. i. 15-20 only eight need to be omitted in order to leave the paragraph without any substantially Christian content. Dr. Schweizer draws attention to two exactly balanced triplets, which form the backbone of the paragraph, and are simply Hellenistic (or Hellenistic-Jewish) in their contents:

He is the image of the invisible God, the first-born of all
        creation;
    for in him were all things created, in heaven and on earth;
    through him and unto him were all things created.

[1] 'Eine urchristliche Taufliturgie', in *Festschrift Rudolf Bultmann* (Stuttgart and Cologne, 1949), pp. 133-48; reprinted in *Exegetische Versuche und Besinnungen*, I (Göttingen, 1960), pp. 34-51.

[2] 'Die Kirche als Leib Christi in den paulinischen Antilegomena', in *Theologische Literaturzeitung*, 86 (1961), cols. 241-56, especially (for Col. i. 15-20) 241-6.

[3] Indeed, neither takes Colossians to be a genuine Pauline letter. I am not convinced of this, though the case for non-Pauline authorship is stronger than it is often felt in England to be. The point is not (in the present argument) of the first importance. The editing of earlier material which appears to have been done, if it was not done by Paul himself, was done in such a way as to represent and indeed to crystallize his attitude to the issues raised.

He is the beginning, the first-born from the dead,
  for in him all the fullness was pleased to dwell,
    through him and unto him to reconcile all things.

This piece of verse (according to Dr. Schweizer) had already before its use in Colossians, been referred to Christ by the insertion of the triplet:

And he it is who is before all things,
And all things have their being in him,
And he it is who is the head of the body.

This triplet asserts that the lost unity of the Cosmos (for which the term 'body' stands) has been recovered in Christ.

According to Dr. Käsemann, the non-Christian, gnostic material had been Christianized into a baptismal hymn. The context as a whole (he says) suggests this. Col. i. 13, with the words 'the Son of his love' ($ὁ$ $υἱὸς$ $τῆς$ $ἀγάπης$ $αὐτοῦ$), suggests the baptism of Christ himself (cf. Mark i. 11, 'My Son the beloved' ($ὁ$ $υἱός$ $μου$ $ὁ$ $ἀγαπητός$)); deliverance out of darkness into light, the inheritance, forgiveness, redemption—all are baptismal themes. The baptismal hymn is adduced in the present passage, which envisages the Colossian heresy, not in order to represent Christ as the chief of the cosmic powers, for this the heretics already believed, but in order to recall the Church to its baptismal confession, and in particular to insist that the only way to the new creation is (not gnostic speculation but) the forgiveness of sins.

Dr. Schweizer regards as interpretative glosses all those fragments of Col. i. 15-20 which have not already been used in the nine lines given above. These have the effect (in sum) of reinterpreting the word body ($σῶμα$), previously used of the cosmos, so as to apply it to the Church and its mission.

There is no need for us to inquire whether either of these theories can be accepted as a whole. Two points stand out as of fundamental importance, and it seems to me that they have been as nearly demonstrated as one can hope such things may be. It seems highly probable that behind the present text of Colossians lies non-Christian material of a gnostic kind, which the author of Colossians (whoever he may have been) has worked over so as to produce the paragraph as we now have it; and that the motive of the working over was the establishing not of a cosmic world-view or even a cosmic Christology, but of the Christian doctrine of redemption over against gnostic speculation.

The whole paragraph shows a turning away from the cosmological to the eschatological and redemptive. The setting is determined by verses 13, 14. These may or may not reflect a baptismal context; if they do, the significance of baptism will be that it crystallizes the doctrine of redemption. The important matters (which are specifically referred to, as baptism is not) are deliverance from the power of darkness, transference into the kingdom of Christ, and redemption through his blood, that is, the forgiveness of sins. With verse 21 we are unquestionably back in the same world; indeed, we have reached it already in verse 18, which speaks of the resurrection, and in verse 20, which speaks of the blood of the cross. It is only in verses 15 ff. that truly cosmological interests prevail; and here the intention may be in part to add a cosmic dimension to the doctrine of redemption—he in whom redemption and forgiveness are to be had is no local or temporary figure; but primarily it is to bring the cosmological speculation which was current and too powerful to be simply stopped under the dominance of the person of the historic (or eschatological) Redeemer. How far the terminology had been selected and the material put together in the Colossian situation it would not be easy to say; our main concern, however, is not with the literary processes by which the text reached its present form but with the theological significance of what is said in it. The opening words (verse 15) suggest the creation of primal man; and in fact it may be said that it is here that we find Paul's equivalent for the doctrine that Philo draws out of the earlier of the two Genesis stories of the creation of man.[1] The primal man is both God's making, and an archetype of creation; he stands as it were on both sides of the gulf between Creator and creation. He is the heavenly pattern on the basis of which empirical man is made. As such,

[1] See p. 75.

he is an instrument of revelation. This is the meaning of 'image', for when εἰκών is followed by ἀόρατος (invisible), it suggests not so much the anthropology of the biblical creation narrative as a means of making known what is otherwise unknown. 'First-born', πρωτότοκος, conceals a well-known linguistic ambiguity, which should probably be handled in the same way as Rom. i. 4 and Phil. ii. 5-11.[1] Its meaning is mobile, and is on the way from 'first-made creation' to a 'being prior to and therefore different from creation'.

In Col. i. 16 ff. it is important to note what is clearly implied though it is never stated. What is *stated* is that the various heavenly bodies, seen and unseen, thrones, lordships, principalities, authorities,[2] were created through Christ and for Christ, the primal Man. What is not stated is what has happened to them *since* creation. The answer to this question comes out in i. 20, where it is said that all things are reconciled through Christ, who made peace through the blood shed on the cross, and in ii. 15, where it is said that in the cross Christ triumphed over the principalities and authorities and openly put them to shame. Now no one reconciles or triumphs over what is not opposed to him; i. 20 and ii. 15 make no sense unless we may suppose that powers that were created for subordination to the heavenly Man have rebelled, and deserted their appointed rank. As rebels, they have been overcome and reconciled[3] in the cross; overcome and reconciled, yet not finally destroyed or appeased, since it is evident that they continue to be inimical to man and his interests. This latter aspect of the matter, however, which is clearly in view in, for example, Rom. viii. 38 f., is not stressed in Col. i. 18 ff., or in ii. 15, where the emphasis lies on the ultimate goal.[4]

We have here, on a different scale, that same picture that we have observed elsewhere. Creation was made subject to man,

---

[1] See pp. 70 ff.

[2] This proliferation of names strongly suggests gnostic origin for the list.

[3] These two words are not fully consistent, but the problem of their inconsistency need not be discussed here. See pp. 115 ff.

[4] It is probable that there is already a reference to reconciliation and restoration in verse 17, for συνέστηκε probably (though not certainly) implies a putting together of sundered fragments.

but it has got out of hand. In truth, only the heavenly Man can subdue it to himself and act as its lord.

We may now return to our theological question about creation and redemption. It is true that, in Colossians, we find cosmological terms, drawn, for example, from the Wisdom literature, which provide a cosmic setting for Jesus Christ. These have the effect of showing the magnitude and certainty of redemption, though this, it must be noted, consists not in the acquisition of cosmological secrets, but in the forgiveness of sins. By this cosmic setting Christ is shown to be most intimately related to creation (both as process and as result); to both the visible creation (including man), and the invisible (including the heavenly powers). In this situation, as so far described, it would be quite true to say that the Agent of creation was manifest in his work; an ordered cosmos would bear witness to him who ordered it. This situation, however, has ceased to exist. When and how it ceased to exist is not stated; but it is clear that if the powers and the rest of creation had remained in him in whom they were created there would have been no necessity to speak (in Col. i. 20) of cosmic reconciliation. The ordered universe is now disordered, and has reached such a pitch of rebellion that he who is the image of the invisible God—Wisdom, Word, Torah, Urmensch, Microcosmos, call him what you will—can only retrieve the situation by shedding his blood and overcoming the power of death by experiencing it. This means that the work of the heavenly Man can be apprehended not in creation as it now exists, but only in the process of redemption. As soon as Paul has said what needs to be said on cosmology in order to bring cosmology into the only setting in which it is intelligible, and to show that when he speaks of redemption and forgiveness he is not speaking of minor irrelevancies, he returns to the sphere in which the work of Christ can be seen and known:

You, who formerly were alienated and enemies in your understanding on account of your wicked works, he has now reconciled in the body of his flesh through death (i. 21 f.).

The cosmos, then, can show only a disordered and distorted picture of the intention of God; it is in the historic figure of Christ that the truth is to be seen, for in Christ, crucified and risen, reconciliation has taken place, or rather has been adumbrated, since it still awaits completion. Christ is the firstborn from the dead (πρωτότοκος ἐκ τῶν νεκρῶν); the firstfruit is the promise of the crop, but it is not the crop; what is true of Christ is not yet true of all men.

2 This last observation suggests the second of the two theological questions that have to be dealt with. This is the problem of eschatology and of myth. Again and again in our study of Pauline Christology we have been brought face to face with a pattern of thought which must be described as eschatological and mythical. This is particularly so in the last paragraph we have studied, Col. i. 15-20, though it is by no means confined to this passage, but is equally to be found in certainly genuine letters —see, for example, Rom. viii. 38 f. There is a creation-myth which involves a demiurge conceived on the pattern of the divine Wisdom of Judaism, or of Philo's primal Man. He bears the image of the invisible God, and thus reveals him, and is himself responsible for the production of the cosmos, whose lord he is. His lordship extends not only over the visible creation, but also over the invisible celestial powers. Differently involved in creation is the first man, Adam, who is never said by Paul to bear the image of God, though he is entrusted with a minor sovereignty, over the animals. This Adam, seduced by Satan, sought to gain the larger divine life above him. This discontent, issuing in rebellion, was not merely a personal fall from grace, but involved also the dragging of humanity as a whole into the service of the elements (στοιχεῖα), who seized their opportunity to gain effective control over God's world.

From this state of bondage and corruption neither the faith of Abraham nor the law of Moses availed to deliver mankind, though each pointed to the relationship with God for which man was created. God himself, however, had appointed a time for the overthrow of the cosmic powers, and when the due moment came he sent forth his Son (Gal. iv. 4), born of a woman (and thus a sharer in the common lot of mortal humanity), born under the law (and thus a participant in that most desperate situation, in which evil powers had seized upon the word of God himself, and twisted it to their own ends). The Son of God, who made his appearance in that very physical human frame which had passed under the dominion of sin (Rom. viii. 3), died on the cross, and then was raised by God from the dead.

So far it is possible to tell a reasonably simple and intelligible story. Difficulty arises when we attempt to evaluate the meaning of the death and resurrection of Jesus, and to describe what happened next, and what is yet to happen. Clearly, Paul was convinced that the death and resurrection of Jesus constituted the overthrow of the evil cosmic powers; yet, though he can speak in terms of a triumphal procession, it is equally evident that the powers of evil are not yet finished with. Death still holds the field, and will be defeated as the last enemy (I Cor. xv. 26); the word 'last' presumably means that others are yet to be destroyed before it is death's turn. But Christ reigns, and one by one his enemies will be placed under his feet, until, on man's behalf, he has recovered the sovereignty for which man was created, and those who are in him (ἐν Χριστῷ) will regain their appointed privileges and dominion, and be related to God as God always intended that men should be. With this consummation is connected the idea of a return of Christ from heaven, where he now is, together with the resurrection of the dead, the transformation of those still living, and the 'wrath to come', from which those who are in Christ will be delivered.

The eschatological element in this story seems to me to make a consistent whole. It has been not infrequently discussed, and there is at this stage little to add to what has already been said. It is of the essence of Paul's thought that the eschatology is partly, but only partly, realized—the futurist eschatology is not to be dismissed as an unfortunate hang-over from the primitive Church—and it remains for Christians to work out their new existence, under the guidance of the Holy Spirit, in a strange interim period, 'between the times'. This is a theme I shall take up in the next chapter.

We cannot, however, fail to note that Paul's story of the Redeemer and the redeemed does not simply contain a mythical element; it is mythical through and through. The attempt to demythologize the myth is another matter that will come into the next chapter, but it must be taken into account here. If the argument that we have followed hitherto is correct, the Pauline mythology can be partly rationalized in anthropological terms, but only partly. Only partly, for Paul himself works out an anthropological dialectic of faith and works, and yet is capable of leaving alongside it the full range of mythical language, as if to indicate that an existential account of man is not adequate, and that his 'principalities and powers' must be taken seriously and objectively. But what does it mean to take them seriously and objectively? It cannot mean less than the recognition that there exist cosmical conditions and circumstances which actively engender sin, suffering, and death, circumstances which are so far anthropological that their existence is due to the fact that man has abandoned his appointed standing in creation. It is naturally possible to believe in the objectivity of these conditions and circumstances without believing in their personality; and it is also possible to see that so far as the human conditions for their existence have ceased to be —that is, as Paul would say, *in Christ*—these forces have lost their strength and grip, though they still prey even upon those who are in Christ until the time comes when they share his resurrection.

One more question, of a different kind, may be raised in this chapter. For at least four Christians, whom we may, without argument, name Matthew, Mark, Luke, and John, the name 'Jesus Christ' suggested the recounting of incidents in which he took part, and the recording of his sayings. Paul did not think of Jesus Christ in this way; of the rich current of gospel tradition he takes only the smallest notice. Why? It is not that he did not believe in the 'historical Jesus'.[1] Undoubtedly he

[1] II Cor. v. 16 does not imply disbelief in the historical existence of Jesus.

did so. The answer must be sought elsewhere; indeed, it has already been hinted at, and may now be made a little more precise.

The story of Jesus as a man could only recount that which he had in common with many other men, for example, the obedience to and trust in God that he shared with Abraham. In his teaching he could only, with perhaps more insight than Moses, urge upon his hearers the claim of God, and declare the approach of the new eschatological day, which, Paul knew, had now dawned. It was not his birth but his death, and above all his resurrection, that had actually ushered in the new day. Emphasis upon the detailed content of the gospel tradition (supposing Paul to have known it) could therefore in Paul's situation have been dangerously misleading. To say this is not to say that we could dispense with the traditions of the life of Jesus. It is in fact (as Paul may have tacitly assumed) the existence of these traditions that makes the Pauline dogmatics credible. This is not because the tradition contains a number of trustworthy stories that show us exactly what Jesus was like and what he really thought about himself and his ministry, and justify Paul's Christological statements, but because it makes it possible to visualize in historical terms the mythological figure who is the centre of Paul's account of God's dealings with men. Paul himself could afford to be content with a bare assertion of the realization in historical and personal terms, that is, in Jesus, of the eschatological myth of salvation. In a later generation this bare assertion did not suffice; this is why we have gospels. And the gospels achieve the same goal as Paul, though they achieve it in a completely different—and, we may add, indispensable—way. Like him, they bind together the anthropological-existential with the mythical-eschatological aspect of salvation. For further discussion of this theme I must point to the next chapter.

# V

# THE MAN TO COME

THE title of this chapter is taken from a passage discussed in the first. In Rom. v. 14 Paul declares that Adam is τύπος τοῦ μέλλοντος, which I have ventured to translate,[1] 'a type of the Man to come', for ὁ μέλλων may be taken as a Pauline equivalent for the expression ὁ ἐρχόμενος (the Coming One), which we meet with elsewhere in the New Testament. The equivalence may remind us that though in Rom. v. 14 Paul was certainly thinking of the historic figure of the incarnate Christ his thought need not have been, and probably was not, confined to the Christ who has come; it may, and probably does, include also the Christ who is yet to come. Relative to Adam, Christ is the 'Man to come', whether we think of the coming described in the gospels, or of his *parousia* in glory.

Paul is interested in nothing less than the whole story of mankind from beginning to end, for the whole story stands under the righteous and merciful design of God. No part of it, in the past, the present, or the future, is outside the scope of his providence. Notwithstanding the grim reality of the struggle against the powers of evil, Paul would have agreed with Wesley:

> In vain doth Satan rage his hour,
> Beyond his chain he cannot go.

In this book we have traced the story from its beginning, when Man upset the balance of God's creation by reaching for that which was above him, for which he had not been made and was not fitted. Out of this unbalance arise both the anthropological and the cosmical *malaise* of the universe: man attempts

[1] *Romans*, pp. 109, 113.

to live independently of his Creator, treating himself as his own
god, and thereby not only ceases to be truly himself but also
loses control of what should have been under his dominion,
and falls under the sway of demonic powers. There are partial
attempts to rectify the position. In Abraham we see a partial
restoration of the anthropological situation, because Abraham
gave God his trust and obedience, and this was counted to him
as righteousness; that is, God took it as ground for giving
Abraham a positive relation to himself, equivalent to that of
man in his primal innocence. Under Moses an act of deliverance took place which Old Testament writers themselves compared with the mythological drama in which God defeated the
forces of chaos, and so established his creation.[1] But Abraham
had had no power to retrieve the cosmic situation; and the
deliverance under Moses had been local, partial, and fundamentally social and political; it had led, moreover, to a worsen-
ing of the anthropological situation, because the cosmic powers
of wickedness had taken the opportunity of perverting law into
legalism. Pointers to the divine act of deliverance and restitu-
tion thus existed, but the act itself, and the agent, were still
awaited.

It was in Jesus Christ that God, when the appointed moment
came, affirmed his promises. Jesus Christ is the Man to come,
and he has come. This assertion, fundamental as it is to the New
Testament, must, however, be qualified in two ways. First,
Jesus' obedient life, which reversed and more than counter-
balanced the sin of Adam, was the life of one man only. No
other, not his closest disciple, achieved the same relation with
God; indeed, the very failure of his disciples even to behave
like decently faithful friends underlines his uniqueness and
isolation. It was not, however, God's intention, as the Old
Testament no less than the New asserts, to restore one human
life only, but humanity; not a man, but Man—Adam, 'ādām.
The work of Jesus, though complete in itself, required extension
and completion in space. Secondly, though in his death and
resurrection Jesus achieved a victory over the cosmic powers of

---

[1] See, *e.g.*, Isa. li. 9 ff.; Ps. lxxxix. 11.

evil, this victory, though decisive, is not yet complete. Not all his enemies have yet been put under his feet. Satan himself continues to be active, so that we are not ignorant of his devices. Evil powers are still in existence which, if they were permitted, would separate men from God's love. The demonic elements (the στοιχεῖα τοῦ κόσμου) are still at work, so that it is possible for Christians to fall back under their dominion, and thus to fall from grace. The historic work of Jesus thus requires extension and completion in time.

It thus remains for what was done in the person of Jesus to be applied to mankind at large; for the running battle that follows a decisive action to be completed in the final overthrow and subjugation of the demonic forces who, since the fall of Adam, have dominated not only the human scene but the cosmos as a whole, which sighs inarticulately for the day when it shall be released from bondage to Vanity, the No-God, and resume the freedom of service to Man.

What this means is that Paul was concerned with an eschatological process. Like other Jews of his day, he looked for the moment when the Lord should descend from heaven, accompanied by the hosts of his holy ones—the plurality of beings who share his holiness and enjoy his victory. Unlike his non-Christian compatriots, however, Paul believed that the eschatological process had already begun. The Christ had already appeared, and had won his cosmic victory in precisely those circumstances of humiliation and obscurity which were necessary if he were to give mankind a new start with the Godward orientation in which man's true life exists. It was necessary that he should live the life of a servant and even pass through the darkness of a hopeless death, deserted by God himself, if he were to be utterly obedient and completely trustful, and it was in consequence of this sacrificial obedience that he had been exalted above all beings in heaven, on earth, and under the earth. In virtue of this exaltation, Christ now reigned at the right hand of God, and the progress of the Gospel propagated eschatological conditions.

Rom. i. 16 ff.: I am not ashamed of the Gospel, for it is the power of God unto salvation [an eschatological term] to every one who believes. For in it God's righteousness [an eschatological term] is now being revealed (ἀποκαλύπτεται, present tense) from faith unto faith. . . . For God's wrath [an eschatological term] is being revealed (ἀποκαλύπτεται). . . .

There are many such assertions of continuing eschatological activity, unfolding in the present in the course of the Church's mission. For example,

II Cor. ii. 14 ff.: Thanks be to God who always leads us in triumph in Christ, and manifests through us in every place the odour of his knowledge. For we are a sweet savour of Christ unto God in every place, among those who are being saved and among those who are perishing; to the one an odour from death unto death, to the other an odour from life unto life.

Consideration of facts such as these marks out the task that still awaits completion. It is not enough to speak of Christ in his incarnate life, or even to add a reference to a future personal manifestation of him. We must look at the period in which the eschatology is in process of realization, the partial fulfilment on the plane of history of the Man to come. At the beginning of the process stands the manifestation of the Son of man, at the end, the completion of the new humanity in him. Between lies a stretch of what can only be described as eschatological history.

We should reach a similar conclusion if we began, as it were, at the other end, and considered a number of important Pauline words and phrases. None is more central and pervasive than the phrase *in Christ* (ἐν Χριστῷ). It is evident that the entire life of the Christian, from beginning to end, is lived in Christ. It is in Christ that men have their existence from God (I Cor. i. 30). Through the Gospel, Paul begot his Corinthian converts in Christ Jesus (I Cor. iv. 15). There is no condemnation for those who are in Christ Jesus (Rom. viii. 1). When Christians are dead, they are the dead in Christ (I Thess. iv. 16). It is immediately clear from these and many other passages that the

Christian life as Paul conceives it is not simply one religious possibility among many others that men might conceivably select for themselves. It exists only in the existence of Christ. The question of the precise sense of the preposition *in*, which has been debated at great length, need not be discussed here. It suffices to remark that men are related to God, and participate in the last things (such as judgement, righteousness, and life), only in virtue of their relation with Christ. The light that this all-embracing term throws upon the Christian life as Paul understood it shows at once (*a*) that there is an expansion of the divine purpose from Christ to humanity at large, and (*b*) that in him men are integrated into an eschatological process.

Again, we might consider the use of the term *body* (σῶμα) in the Pauline letters. The one word passes through a range of meanings, and there are passages where it is difficult to place it within this range.[1] It may refer simply to the body of Christ's flesh, the human, material body that experienced death on the cross, or to any other human body. This, however, is certainly not the only sense in which the word is used. In Rom. xii and I Cor. xii 'body' becomes the basis of a metaphor that describes the Church, an organism containing many interrelated members. In Rom. xii. 5 Paul declares that 'we who are many are one body in Christ'. The 'body' metaphor is brought into close relation with the 'in Christ' formula, to which it adds a significant truth: those who are in Christ are in him not only as individuals but as—a body. In I Cor. xii. 27 he says (with little or no difference in meaning), 'You are the body of Christ, and severally members of it'. In Col. i. 18 the metaphor has developed, possibly under the influence of the notion of the cosmos as a body,[2] so that Christ is spoken of as the head of the body. This does not mean that Christ is part of the community on equal terms with the rest; the body is his body, and as head he is head and lord over it. Further exposition is not called for

---

[1] See J. A. T. Robinson, *The Body* (London, 1952), and E. Schweizer, in *Theologische Literaturzeitung*, 86 (1961), cols. 161-74, and 241-56.
[2] See pp. 83 f.; it must be regarded as at least possible that this development is not due to Paul himself, but, understood as in the text, the new thought is not inconsistent with Paul's doctrine.

here; all that need be noted is that the word *body* leads us out
from the one historic man Jesus to a plurality of men, a
community.

Another important term is *image* (εἰκών). It might be expected that this word should be used, in dependence on Gen. i,
with reference to the creation of Adam, or perhaps to Christ
as the last Adam. It is true that in two places (II Cor. iv. 4; Col.
i. 15) Christ is said to be the image of God, but in these the
context of thought is not creation but revelation (on Col. i. 15
see pp. 85 f.). As the 'image' Christ is the means by which the
invisible God is revealed. The figure of Wisdom is in the background. The remaining passages (excluding Rom. i. 23; I Cor.
xi. 7, which are not relevant) in which 'image' is used form a
striking set.

Rom. viii. 29: Those whom [God] foreknew, he also pre-
destinated to share the image borne by his Son (σνμμόρφους
τῆς εἰκόνος τοῦ νἱοῦ αὐτοῦ), that he might be [not the one
Son of God but] the eldest of a large family of brothers.

I Cor. xv. 49: As we have borne the image of the earthy
man [Adam], we shall bear[1] also the image of the heavenly
Man [Christ].

II Cor. iii. 18: As we all, with unveiled face, behold as in
a mirror the glory of the Lord, we are transformed into the
same image, from glory to glory.

Col. iii. 9 ff.: You have put off the old man with his deeds,
and put on the new man who is renewed with a view to
knowledge in the image of him that created him, where there
cannot be Greek and Jew, circumcision and uncircumcision,
barbarian, Scythian, bond, free, but Christ is all and in all.

These passages show clearly that the term 'image' does not
relate to Christ alone. He *is* the image of God, and men bear his
image, so that he no longer stands alone, but as the eldest of a
large family. More correctly, we should say that men *will* bear
his image, for the word sends us out from the solitary figure
of the historical Jesus not simply to a multiplicity of men (extension and fulfilment in space) but also into the eschatological

[1] See p. 76, n. 1.

future (extension and fulfilment in time): We shall bear the image of the heavenly Adam. With this hope should be compared a further passage, Phil. iii. 20 f.:

> We await as saviour the Lord Jesus Christ, who shall transform the body of our humiliation, and make it share the form (σύμμορφον, cf. Rom. viii. 29) of the body of his glory, according to the active power (ἐνέργειαν) by which he is able to subject all things to himself (cf. I Cor. xv. 24-8).

This eschatology of the new man and the image of God is, like all New Testament eschatology, no simple futurist eschatology, for it is brought into the present—we are now being transformed (μεταμορφούμεθα, II Cor. iii. 18); yet, as all the passages make clear, what happens in the present is an anticipation of that which properly belongs to the future. Like *body* (σῶμα), *image* (εἰκών) leads our thought from Christ to the Church; it also leads it on to the final destiny of mankind.

The result of renewal in the image of Christ is the formation of the 'new man', which may be thought of as a special case of the 'new creation' (II Cor. v. 17). As well as the terms 'old man', 'new man', Paul uses another pair, 'outward man', 'inward man'. The whole complex is worthy of study, but is much too complicated to be treated in detail here.

> Rom. vi. 6: Our old man (ὁ παλαιὸς ἡμῶν ἄνθρωπος) has been crucified with Christ.
>
> vii. 22: I approve of the law of God so far as the inward man is concerned (κατὰ τὸν ἔσω ἄνθρωπον).
>
> II Cor. iv. 16: Our outward man (ὁ ἔξω ἡμῶν ἄνθρωπος) is disintegrating (διαφθείρεται), but our inward man (ὁ ἔσω ἡμῶν) is being renewed day by day.
>
> Col. iii. 9 ff.: You have put off the old man with his deeds, and put on the new man who is renewed with a view to knowledge in the image of him that created him, where there cannot be Greek and Jew, circumcision and uncircumcision, barbarian, Scythian, bond, free, but Christ is all and in all.

In these passages, the 'new' or 'inward man' is not precisely Christ, as objectively distinct from the believer, nor, at the other extreme, is it a new nature, mystically or sacramentally bestowed upon and received by the believer, which he henceforth objectively and personally possesses. The terms, though applied primarily to the individual Christian, nevertheless (as Col. iii. 11 shows) point also to the new community. Like the word 'image', they direct us to that place where the individual and corporate hope of mankind meet in the future in Christ. For Paul, 'Man' is a historical and individual term, for Jesus of Nazareth, who lived in Palestine in the first half of the first century and was crucified under Pontius Pilate, was the Man to come. But the same word is also an eschatological and collective term, for it denotes the new humanity that is to be in Christ, and is already partially and inadequately adumbrated in Christians. The full conception of the Man to come can be disclosed only at the last day, when the heavenly Man appears with the holy ones who are conformed to his image.

There is thus a good deal in the epistles to suggest that Paul viewed the preaching of the Gospel, and the building up of the churches founded under its influence, as a part of the process of eschatology, and a practical though partial realization of the universal significance of the person and action of Jesus Christ. In this chapter it must be our task to study Paul's understanding of the Christian, the Church, and the world in this eschatological setting; but first we must do a little more to illuminate the setting itself.

We may do this by studying Paul's use of the term 'kingdom' (βασιλεία). He appears to distinguish between the kingdom of God, and the kingdom of Christ (to which he refers only twice). The kingdom of God most often refers plainly to the future. There is a group of passages which speak of *inheriting* the kingdom of God:

> I Cor. vi. 9 f.: The unrighteous shall not inherit God's kingdom . . . thieves shall not inherit God's kingdom.
> xv. 50: Flesh and blood cannot inherit God's kingdom.
> Gal. v. 21: Those who practise such things shall not inherit God's kingdom.

A few other passages refer with equal clearness to the future:

> I Thess. ii. 12: . . . who calls us into his own kingdom and glory.
> II Thess. i. 5: . . . that you may be counted worthy of the kingdom of God [that is, of attaining to it].

There are three passages where the time reference is less clear:

> Rom. xiv. 17: The kingdom of God is not eating and drinking, but righteousness, peace, and joy in the Holy Spirit.
> I Cor. iv. 20: The kingdom of God does not consist in speech, but in power.
> Col. iv. 11: These men only are my fellow-workers for the kingdom of God.

The last is not conclusive, but probably means both that Paul and his fellow-workers carry out their mission with reference to the future kingdom, and also that their work is done in the power of the kingdom operating in the present. This thought —of the partial anticipation in the present of the future kingdom—is common in the New Testament, and probably lies behind Rom. xiv. 17 and I Cor. iv. 20 also. In the former of these, the reference to the Holy Spirit (whose work it is, for Paul, as for other New Testament writers, to bring future eschatological conditions into the present) should be noted; in the latter, the key[1] is the allusion to iv. 8. There are Corinthians who claim to have come already to the kingdom (ἐβασιλεύσατε); well, this may be so; but the test of it is not what they say, but what they can do. Where the Spirit is truly at work, anticipating the reign of God in Christian life and the work of evangelism, there righteousness, peace, joy, and power are to be seen. In the work of the Spirit, the kingdom of God may be said to be proleptically present though it remains essentially future.

One reference to the kingdom of Christ is unambiguously present in its bearing:

---

[1] See J. Weiss, *Der erste Korintherbrief* (*Kritisch-Exegetischer Kommentar über das Neue Testament*, 9th edition, Göttingen, 1910), p. 121.

18|31

Col. i. 13: . . . who rescued us from the power of darkness, and transferred us into the kingdom of the Son of his love.

Only one passage, but that the most significant, remains:

I Cor. xv. 23-8: But each one shall be raised in his own order (τάγμα): Christ as firstfruits, then, at his coming (παρουσία), those who belong to Christ. Then follows the End, when he delivers up the kingdom to his God and Father, when he does away with every principality, and every authority and power. For he must go on reigning in his kingdom (βασιλεύειν) until he places all his enemies under his feet (Ps. cx. 1). As the last enemy, death is destroyed; for he has subjected all things under his feet (Ps. viii. 7). But when he says, 'All things have been subjected', it is clear that this is with the exception of him who subjected all things to him. But when all things are subjected to him, then the Son himself too shall be subjected to him who subjected all things to him, that God may be all in all.

In this paragraph, Paul asserts that Christ will exercise kingship for a limited time, during which his enemies will be forced one by one to submit to him, so that in him Man will regain the lordship (even over death) that was originally entrusted to him. At the end of this period, Christ will hand over the kingdom to God the Father. This is stated in verse 24, and repeated in other words in verse 28. We cannot from verse 24 deduce an interval (accommodating what has been called a *Zwischenreich*, or 'Intervening Kingdom') between the *parousia* and the End (τέλος); it seems rather that the End is thought of as following directly upon the *parousia*, the signal by which it is introduced. Christ's reign is thus placed not between his *parousia* and some 'end' distinct from this, but between his resurrection and the *parousia*; that is, during the period of the Church's activity on earth. The kingdom of Christ is thus a preliminary and chronologically limited reign. It exists as the necessary prelude to the moment when Christ himself is duly subordinated to God the Father, and the kingdom of *God* is fully realized and established. Creation, and Christ himself, attain the ultimate purpose of their existence only when God is all in all. It was precisely the denial of this supremacy of God that was responsible for the fall, for the subjugation of man to the creation which he should have ruled, and for the distortion of his own nature; full restoration is accordingly possible only on the basis of 'God all in all'.

This last observation suggests the sense in which these difficult verses (24, 28) are to be understood. They are difficult in the sense that it is not easy to accommodate them to the Trinitarian orthodoxy that developed in the following centuries. It should not be too quickly assumed that this orthodoxy is in all respects correct, and that difficult New Testament passages should be tailored to fit it. Greek orthodoxy was too static, metaphysical, and ontological to do full justice to the mobility and dynamic of biblical thought, which does not deal so much in essential relationships as in transaction and achievement. It must be remembered that in this paragraph Paul is dealing with that which man has lost—through man; and with that which he has gained—through man.

> By man came death; by man came also the resurrection of the dead. For as in Adam all die, even so in Christ shall all be made alive (I Cor. xv. 21 f.).

Christ is the Son of God, but he is also the incorporation of mankind; as the incorporation of mankind he is destined in the restoring mercy of God to reign once more over all creation and over all his enemies, including eventually death; but he can so reign only in his readiness to submit himself completely to God, and indeed in the concrete actualization of this readiness. It was refusal to render this submission to God that cost Adam, and mankind in him, his life; it is the rendering of it by mankind in Christ that leads to victory over death. After the resurrection as before it, Christ realizes his glory, and is the *Lord* (Phil. ii. 11), in humble obedience and self-abnegation. It is precisely in these terms of humility and obedience, and in no other terms whatever, that the eschatology is being realized, and the new Man created in the image of Christ built up.

It is this theme that we must now work out, in relation to

the Individual, the Church, and the World.

1. *The New Creation and the Individual.*—The place to begin is Paul's doctrine of justification.[1] The groundwork of this is eschatological. Justification means God's act of doing justice and judgement; of pronouncing sentence in his court, and especially of giving the verdict of acquittal for those whom it is right that he should acquit. Every Jew knew where and when one might expect to see God doing justice: in the great assize at the last day, when final and irrevocable doom would be pronounced. We shall not now trace in detail the process of thought, and especially the understanding of the death of Christ, which made it possible for Paul to assert that this last judgement had been anticipated, and that the man who was prepared humbly and obediently to hear and accept God's judgement, that is, to hear it in faith, could, to his own astonishment, hear not the fully deserved verdict of 'Convicted' but the completely undeserved verdict of 'Acquitted' (which is not the same as 'innocent'). Rather, we must underline two further points.

(*a*) The hearing of faith (which is certainly not an attitude that man is able of himself freely to adopt, but is a gift from God, made possible in the Holy Spirit) is itself a reversal of the rebellious dissatisfaction of Adam, who was not content to accept the place God assigned him, but set out to secure a better place for himself. One might almost say, not simply that justification is through faith, but that faith *is* justification. This is the ultimate ground of the *sola fide*, and the reason why this is and must continue to be a criterion of theology and of Christian life. It is not that faith is in Pauline or any other proper usage a shibboleth, or an 'Open Sesame' which operates as a magic formula. It is not even that faith is an indispensable agent or instrument which by itself effects justification or salvation. It is simply that faith is a description (from the human side) of the relationship with God for which God created man, in which man lets God truly be God, and lets himself truly be man, that is, the obedient creature of the loving God. Now the

[1] See *Romans*, pp. 74 ff., and index *s.v.*

only way into this relationship of faith is—faith. No man can create a relationship of complete dependence upon God by that which he can achieve independently of God; nor can he so sustain it. This truth (that faith is, as it were, both means and end) is reflected in the variety of ways in which the word is used in the Pauline letters. Out of many passages Rom. xi. 20 may be quoted: It is by your faith that you stand (σὺ δὲ τῇ πίστει ἔστηκας; the point here is in the *standing*).[1]

(*b*) Justification is an anticipation of God's verdict at the last judgement. The last judgement itself leads to the heavenly life. The anticipated verdict leads to an anticipation of the heavenly life. This can only be described as a progressive realization of the conditions for which God created man, that is, a life of communion with himself, and of dominion over the rest of creation; a life of holiness and of bliss. It must never be forgotten that in the present age this heavenly life is truly anticipated, but only anticipated. The evil powers, though their decisive defeat has already taken place, retain their capacity for inflicting harm and pain, and for leading astray. Death still reigns, and will continue to do so till the *parousia* and the End. Christians, including not least the apostles (I Cor. iv. 9–13), are constantly in peril from demonic forces, though they are assured that these cannot separate them from God's love (Rom. viii. 38 f.). Nevertheless, though the anticipation is partial and must be qualified by the observation that the justified man continues to live in the present age, it is also real, and being real imposes an obligation upon those who enjoy it.

Rom. vi. 11–14: [Since Christ has died to sin, once for all,] so do you also consider that you yourselves are dead to sin, but alive to God in Christ Jesus. Let not sin reign in your mortal body so that you obey your body's desires. Do not offer your members to sin, as weapons in the service of unrighteousness, but offer yourselves to God as dead men brought to life, and offer him your members as weapons in

---

[1] Rom. v. 2 would be a particularly good example if the long text (including the words τῇ πίστει) could be accepted; but this is doubtful. There is, however, no lack of material.

the service of righteousness. For sin shall not dominate (κυριεύσει, future) over you.

Our discussion of I Cor. xv. 24, 28 will be recalled. Christ's own glory is fulfilled in his submission to the Father; the anticipated glory of the Christian life is realized in the same submission.

From this point we may take a further step, in which the two observations (a) and (b) come together in a single aspect of Christian life.

The basic terms in which Christian existence must be understood are eschatological. It rests upon Christ's own resurrection and victory over the powers brought forward from the time of the End, and upon the verdict of acquittal brought forward from the last judgement. It is thus a unique eschatology, since it asserts that, notwithstanding appearances, the End has already come, and further that, notwithstanding this confident assertion, the End is not yet. Out of this formula 'Already—Not yet', which is the fundamental pattern of the Christian life, we see evolving in Paul the more developed maxim of 'As if not' (ὡς μή).[1] The substance of this we have already encountered in the 'consider' (λογίζεσθε) of Rom. vi. 11. The Roman Christians are manifestly not living the resurrection life of freedom from sin; they are, however, commanded to live as if they were already free from sin, since in truth it no longer has any claim upon them; to live as if they were not, in this age, under the bondage of sin and death. But the classical passage in which the very words are several times repeated is I Cor. vii. 29 ff. In view of the eschatological situation (ὁ καιρὸς συνεσταλμένος—there is little time left), those who have wives are to be as if they had them not; those who weep, as if they wept not; those who rejoice, as if they rejoiced not; those who buy, as if they did not gain possession; those who have dealings with the world, as if they had no stake in it. This is not an easy passage to understand precisely. J. Weiss (ad loc.; see p. 100, n. 1)

---

[1] Compare R. Bultmann, in *Theologie des Neuen Testaments* (Tübingen, 1948–53), pp. 182, 346 f.; *Man in God's Design* (Newcastle and Valence, 1952), p. 52; *Primitive Christianity in its Contemporary Setting* (London, 1956), p. 207.

claims that here the Stoic[1] ἀταραξία (passiveness) shines through, and Lietzmann (*ad loc.*; see p. 48, n. 1) approves. But this view is rightly criticized by Dr. Kümmel (Lietzmann-Kümmel, p. 178), who points to Rom. xii. 15, 'Rejoice with those who rejoice, weep with those who weep'. Paul is not commending that inward serenity which is undisturbed by the changes and chances of this fleeting world, and especially by the changes and chances that happen to others. The chapter as a whole shows that though he would have been happy enough to see all men like himself, unmarried, he saw in marriage an institution which was (to say no more) for most men a neces-sity; and within it he did not, except for occasional and special purposes, advise abstinence. He is therefore not saying here, Live as a celibate husband. Similarly he is not saying, Do not weep, do not rejoice, do not buy and sell, do not have dealings with the world. His meaning is given by the gospel saying (I do not suggest that Paul was aware of it), Where your treasure is, there shall your heart be also. Once more the situation is illuminated if, for comparison and contrast, we go back to Adam. It was Adam's error that he rooted himself in this world, hiding in it from God. This is the attitude that is reversed in, and is, for the Christian, inconsistent with, faith. The danger of the married state is, Paul teaches, that the married person is more concerned to please his partner than to please God (I Cor. vii. 33 f.); he is here adding the possibility that the married person may in this respect live *as if* he were unmarried. He may thus be free—as the servant of Christ.

With this discussion in mind, we may look at an even more difficult passage, II Cor. vi. 8 ff.:

> . . . as deceivers, and yet true; as unknown, and yet well known; as dying, and behold! we live; as chastened, and yet not put to death; as grieving, yet always rejoicing; as poor, yet making many rich; as having nothing, and possessing all things.

In these verses Paul's meaning shifts. In the first two pairs he is

---

[1] It was surely by an oversight that Weiss wrote 'Stoic' and not 'Epicurean'.

speaking objectively of the estimation in which he is held by various persons. To one he is a deceiver, to another true; to one he is an unknown nobody, by another he is recognized as an apostle of Christ. But this thought, and perhaps the influence of Ps. cxviii. 17 f., lead him further. It is not a matter of varying opinion but of fact that Paul is both dying and living, chastened yet not killed, grieving yet rejoicing, poor yet enriching others, having nothing yet possessing all things. This dialectic is true in the new relationship to God in Jesus Christ, which is determined by crucifixion and resurrection, and by the subordinate position deliberately taken by the exalted Christ.

A particularly important example of the dialectic that grows out of the primitive eschatology is to be found in the doctrine of baptism. On the practical level, it is clear on the one hand that baptism was an institution to which Paul could sit pretty loose. It is hard to make I Cor. i. 17 mean less than this. The prime apostolic function was not baptizing but preaching the Gospel. Doubtless the converts were baptized by someone, but this was not a proceeding in which Paul felt it necessary to take part personally. On the other hand, it is evident that Paul did take it for granted that baptism was a universal practice. Otherwise he would scarcely have expressed himself as in Gal. iii. 27: 'All you who were baptized into Christ' (ὅσοι εἰς Χριστὸν ἐβαπτίσθητε). If this had left out members of the Galatian congregation the argument would have fallen to the ground. This practical attitude—of expecting baptism to take place, but not troubling to do much about it—points to the theological understanding of baptism that underlies Paul's practice.

Discussions of this subject have often taken one or another of two opposite views. According to one, Paul conceived baptism as the efficient cause in salvation. The rite was provided by the Church, and it was effective in cleansing the initiate from sin, and in procuring for him the benefit of dying and rising with Christ; that is, it inaugurated the new life within him. Baptism not only represented but effected burial with the dead Christ, and the man who arose out of the water was the new man alive with Christ. According to the other view, baptism is no more than the symbolic representation and seal of what had already been effected by other means. 'St. Paul saw in Baptism the normal but not necessary, the helpful but not indispensable sign and seal put upon the act of faith appropriating the gift of God in Christ.'[1]

Neither of these views seems to be exactly Paul's own. It will be instructive to make a comparison between baptism and circumcision. That there exists a measure of formal parallelism between the two initiatory rites is clear. Among many profound differences, however, perhaps the greatest is this. Circumcision (with baptism and sacrifice) admitted a proselyte immediately into Judaism; he had at once all that there was in Judaism to have. Christian baptism could effect no such result, not because it was in itself an inferior rite, but because there was nothing comparable to be admitted to. The Church, though it has a visible expression on earth, is not capable of definition in the same simple and self-evident terms as a race, or even a religious organization. The visible expression of it (as we shall see later) can never be more than a preliminary and provisional community, and it follows that baptism into it cannot have the finality and definiteness of the physical rite of admission into Israel after the flesh. Baptism is a concrete and visible expression of the faith that justifies because it allows God to be the creating and justifying God. The man who dies in baptism accepts thereby the sentence of God upon sin which was pronounced historically in the death of Christ; the man who arises from baptism recognizes that the resurrection of Christ is the dawn (though not the full realization) of the new age. This means that baptism is not and cannot be a once-for-all act. As a rite, baptism is not repeated; but unless it is in substance continually renewed it might as well not take place at all. It admits not to a settled and final state of salvation, but to the dialectic of death and resurrection; not to the age to come, but to the interpenetration of this age and the age to come, which becomes actual for the man who dies and rises daily. Of this provisional character of baptism, and of the fact that it does not

[1] C. A. A. Scott, *Christianity according to St. Paul* (Cambridge, 1932), p. 114.

*ex opere operato* admit to full enjoyment of the promise, the baptism of Israel into Moses (I Cor. x. 2), by which the people entered neither into a state of sinlessness nor into the promised land,[1] is the perpetual reminder and warning. To put the matter differently, baptism also is included in the dialectic of ὡς μή, 'as if not'.

It is necessary to see the question of baptism in perspective. The believer (and he must be a believer or he would not seek baptism—this is in itself the death-stroke to all theories that see in baptism the decisive and indispensable beginning of all Christian life) accepts baptism as a sign and means of his entering upon the new creation. Yet he knows that the death and resurrection of baptism do not mean the end of his own earthly existence, and his translation into the perfected life of the age to come. Baptism itself belongs within the intermediate period in which this age and the age to come run concurrently, and it partakes of both, in its action and in its effects. It unites with Christ, who is the victorious Lord, yet is still engaged in conflict with his enemies, and continues even in his exaltation to show the submissive obedience of the cross. Baptism is meaningless if it does not take place within the context of the obedience of faith, by which it is both preceded and followed.[2] It belongs to the *theologia crucis*, not the *theologia gloriae*, and must be worked out in sacrificial obedience and service. Even so, however, it is not fulfilled, it is not even truly confirmed, until the last day.

Baptism forms a suitable transition to our next main theme.

2. *The New Creation and the Church.*—Men are baptized 'into Christ' (Gal. iii. 27). Paul can also say, 'In one Spirit were we all baptized into one body' (I Cor. xii. 13). Paul does not identify Christ with his body, but, as we have seen,[3] the word

---

[1] See pp. 47-50.
[2] It is scarcely necessary to point out that the baptism of infants, a practice Paul nowhere refers to, is not in mind here. On this subject see J. Jeremias, *Infant Baptism in the First Four Centuries* (London, 1960), and K. Aland, *Die Säuglingstaufe im Neuen Testament und in der Alten Kirche* (Theologische Existenz Heute, 86; Munich, 1961).
[3] See pp. 96 f.

σῶμα (body) varies in meaning, and draws attention to the close relation between Christ and those who are in Christ. We have also seen[1] that Christ is the unique seed of Abraham, though in such a way that in him (and not otherwise) the seed (σπέρμα) becomes a true collective noun, since those who by faith are 'in Christ' become, in virtue of this, heirs of Abraham and of the promise. The work of the new Adam is not simply to produce a handful of new individual men, all bearing the image of the heavenly Man, but to produce a new unit of existence, which is as truly one in Christ as the human race as a whole is one in Adam. 'You are all one person (εἷς) in Christ Jesus' (Gal. iii. 28).

No more than his Christology can Paul's doctrine of the Church be fully expounded here. The most we can attempt is to view it from the special standpoint we are employing. The Church, especially in its preaching and at the breaking of bread, proclaims the Lord's death till he shall come; that is, it bears witness to the past act of victory and redemption until the future act of victory and redemption makes such testimony otiose. The Church stands within the dialectic which we have seen to be determinative of Christian life; this is manifestly true as regards its existence in time, but it is true also as regards its extension in space, or scope.

The former point is important, but familiar; it need not be argued, but may be briefly illustrated; first, from the Church's worship, and the exercise therein of spiritual gifts, which are a sign of the Church's life in God, and of the realization of eschatology. It has often been pointed out that the Holy Spirit, described by Paul as *firstfruits* and *earnest* (Rom. viii. 23; II Cor. i. 22; v. 5), is the agency and mark of the eschatological situation of the Church. It constitutes the first instalment of the blessed life, which proves at the same time that the age to come has dawned, and that it has not yet been consummated. God who has already given them the Spirit may be expected and trusted to give men their whole inheritance in due course (Gal. v. 5). The gifts of the Spirit, such as prophecy and speaking

[1] See pp. 76-79.

with tongues, are thus manifest tokens displayed publicly in worship that God has begun to realize his promises. These activities are by no means the whole of the Spirit's work, and spiritual gifts, it has been said,[1] are no more than a parable of the truth; yet a Church without them would cease to be a parable of the truth. Such a Church would lose its right to exist, for it would cease to point beyond itself to God as the meaning of its life. The Church must therefore be careful not to despise prophecy, and it must not forbid, though, for its greater effectiveness, it may bridle, glossolalia.

For a second, related, illustration we may consider the rudimentary developments of ministry in the Pauline letters. I say 'rudimentary', though they are perhaps less rudimentary than what we commonly understand by 'the ministry', since in the Pauline churches it is understood that every member is a minister.[2] And I say 'related', because it is clear that every ministry is dependent upon a spiritual gift. This is as true of the apostles as it is of humbler and less travelled servants of Christ in the Church. The Pauline letters contain no reference to the formal appointment of elders (they do not even contain the word), and it is to be understood that not only those who exercise an evidently 'pneumatic' ministry, such as prophets and those who speak with tongues, but also those who take the lead, or preside, are singled out and equipped by the Spirit rather than appointed in an autocratic or democratic way. I Cor. xvi. 15 is a significant illustration of this. The household of Stephanas 'have appointed themselves (ἔταξαν ἑαυτούς) for ministry to the saints (εἰς διακονίαν τοῖς ἁγίοις)'. This sentence certainly cannot mean that the persons in question have been appointed by some other church authority, whether 'from above' by apostles, or 'from below' by the community; nor does it mean that they set themselves up in an arbitrary and self-willed manner to act as lords over the Church. No other

---

[1] By the late E. C. Hoskyns, in a lecture. I am not aware that he so expressed himself in print. The whole of this paragraph arises out of his remark, though I cannot claim his authority for it.

[2] Cf. I Cor. xii. 7: To *each one* is given a manifestation of the Spirit for mutual profit. Cf. also Rom. xii. 6.

Christian, even Paul, had appointed them, but they had responded to the leading of the Spirit, who had put them forward (in part no doubt for the excellent practical reason that they were the most experienced Christians available) to take the lead in the service of the Corinthian Church. Rom. xii. 8 also takes for granted that presidency is as much a spiritual gift as prophecy, teaching, and exhortation. As the gift of the Spirit, the various ministries by which the Church is served are, like the gifts of inspired speech, a mark of God's presence, and must be valued and respected as such. But Paul never suggests that either in themselves, or by virtue of any form they may take, they can either constitute or guarantee God's presence.

Like the individual Christian, the Church stands under the sign of 'Already—Not yet', which is thought through by Paul into the dialectic of 'As if not'. The Church as the assembly, the ἐκκλησία, of the people of God is never, in his view, an optional adjunct to the Gospel, for what Christ is, he is in relation to humanity at large, and the establishing of the seed of Abraham in him is proper to his work. It was the divine intention that he should be the first-born among many brethren, incorporating in himself the whole company of the heirs of the promise. As the sign of a new humanity the Church is thus part of the eternal purpose of God; but it is the sign, and not the realization of the new humanity. Because it exists within the present age it inevitably takes on visible form, and the Spirit works through specific gifts such as speaking with tongues, showing kindness to the needy, and presiding over church meetings, and these specific gifts are held on behalf of the whole body by particular persons. But the Church may never identify its own form, which is relative to the present age, or the individuals within it who exercise gifts, or even the gifts themselves, with the eternal and completed purpose of God. The Church is truly a means by which God is fulfilling his eschatological purpose; but it is not the fulfilment of this purpose. It follows that the Church must always sit loose to any particular shape it may at any time take, and to the organization it may at any time give to its ministers—that is, its whole membership. All such matters have only provisional significance.[1]

We deal with a more difficult question when we consider the extension of the Church in space, that is, its relation to the whole extent of humanity. Does Paul think that the Gospel will eventually bring all men within its scope, or does he teach that, whether through the eternal decree of God or through their own wise or foolish choice, some men will eventually be saved but others eternally lost? At first sight, it appears that passages can be quoted on each side of this issue. Thus Paul writes in

> Rom. xi. 25 f.: I do not wish you, brethren, to be ignorant of this mystery, lest you become wise in your own estimation, that a partial hardening has befallen Israel until the full total of the Gentiles has come in; so all Israel shall be saved.
>
> v. 18 f.: Therefore, as the result of one act of transgression was condemnation for all, so the result of one act of righteousness was justification leading to life for all; for as through the disobedience of the one man, the mass of men (οἱ πολλοί) were constituted sinners, so also through the obedience of the One, the mass of men shall be constituted righteous.
>
> I Cor. xv. 22: As in Adam all die, so in Christ shall all be made alive.

Particularly important is the parallel drawn between the universal effect of Adam's sin (*all* sin and *all* die), and the effect of Christ's act of righteousness.

But there are other passages; those, for example, which place the saved and the perishing side by side:

> I Cor. i. 18: The word of the cross is foolishness to those who are perishing, but to us who are being saved it is the power of God.
>
> II Cor. ii. 15 f.: We are a sweet savour of Christ unto God, in the saved and in the perishing; to the one an odour from death unto death, to the other an odour from life unto life.

[1] That this was at least partially grasped by others than Paul is shown from a different angle in one of the most distinguished series of Hewett Lectures—B. H. Streeter's *The Primitive Church* (London, 1929)—which demonstrates the variety of 'Church Orders' existing in the sub-apostolic age. Streeter's argument has often been resented, never (so far as I know) refuted.

Gal. vi. 7 f.: Be not deceived, God is not mocked. Whatever a man sows, that shall he also reap. He that sows to his
own flesh shall of the flesh reap destruction; he that sows to
the Spirit shall of the Spirit reap eternal life.

Is it possible to bring these two sets of passages into harmony?
Or must we draw the conclusion that Paul was for ever changing his mind on the subject, as his thought oscillated between
the invincible and universal sovereign grace of God and the
freedom of man to reject the gracious offer of God in Christ?

The apparent universalism of the former set of passages
becomes on investigation far less clear-cut. The 'all Israel' of
Rom. xi. 26 means no more than the same expression in the
Mishnah, where the claim that 'all Israel have a share in the
world to come' is immediately followed by a long list of exceptions.[1] In Rom. v the contrasting parallelism between verses
18 and 19 is to be noted. In verse 19 it is stated that *many*[2] will
be made righteous, that is, justified; in verse 18, where the word
is *all*, there is no verb, and what Paul stresses is the universal
scope or potentiality of Christ's work, not a universalist view
of its results. A similar observation may be made with regard
to I Cor. xv. 21 f. As far as all men are concerned, Adam is the
source of death, Christ the source of life.

The context in which Paul saw his own missionary work
was that of the narrow interval between the resurrection and
the *parousia*. It is in this sense that he writes in Rom. xv. 19 that
he has completed ($\pi\epsilon\pi\lambda\eta\rho\omega\kappa\acute{\epsilon}\nu\alpha\iota$) the Gospel in the eastern and
north-eastern districts of the Mediterranean basin. This
certainly does not mean that Paul has preached to every living
person in the vast area between Jerusalem and Illyricum, still
less that all have become Christians; it means that he has done
all he can expect to do before the *parousia*. For him,[3] the final
gathering in of the Gentiles (and *a fortiori* of the Jews—Rom.

---

[1] See *Romans*, pp. 223 f.

[2] $\pi o\lambda\lambda o\acute{\iota}$, not $\pi\acute{\alpha}\nu\tau\epsilon s$, *all*. It is true that, for Paul, $\pi o\lambda\lambda o\acute{\iota}$, like the Hebrew
*rabbīm*, is contrasted with *one*, not with *all*; but this does not mean that it is
identical with *all*.

[3] As, it seems, for Jesus also. See J. Jeremias, *Jesus' Promise to the Nations*
(London, 1958).

xi. 25 f.) is an eschatological miracle. The mission thus falls within the eschatological period of 'Already—Not yet', the time of Christ's reign in which his adversaries are being overthrown (I Cor. xv. 24 f.), and thus belongs to the category of activities headed 'As if not'. It is right for the apostle and his helpers to strain every nerve in the work of evangelism, and to rejoice over the fruit it bears; but its failure or success must never be identified with the ultimate failure or success of the word of God (cf. Rom. ix. 6). These observations, however, direct us to our third, and last, point.

3. *The New Creation and the World.*—It is important here to remember the position from which Paul sets out. The rebellion of Adam led, as we have seen, to a double consequence: on the one hand, to a distortion of the make-up of human nature, and, on the other, to the subjugation of mankind, and of the cosmos itself, to powers which should have been the servants of man. These powers, which seized upon man's will as their point of attack, and demonstrated their wickedness by making use even of the law, were overthrown by the death and resurrection of Jesus Christ, and, though they did not immediately cease to exist, but rather continue to put up a resistance which can be highly dangerous, they are doomed. But what is their doom? The problem is set us in mythological terms, and we can do no more than speculate about it in mythological terms, but it may be profitable for a moment to do so.

It seems clear that the cosmic elements (τὰ στοιχεῖα τοῦ κόσμου), to which Paul sees fallen man in bondage, and Christian man always in danger of relapsing, are closely connected with the heavenly bodies. Both in Galatians and Colossians they are mentioned in a context which has to do with the calendar—days, months, seasons, feasts, new moons—all institutions that are governed by the regular and dominating motion of sun, moon, planets, and stars. This connection accords with the astrological world-view shared by many of Paul's contemporaries and alluded to by him, whether he believed in it or not. Now sun, moon, planets, and stars are parts of creation, intended for the service of man just as were animals and vegetation (Gen. i. 14-19). In consequence of the fall, the animals which should have been the servants of the Son of man (Ps. viii. 7 f.) became estranged from him, and the earth ceased to give its fruit without the expenditure of toil and sweat; left to itself it produced thorns and thistles (Gen. iii. 17 ff.). The rebellion of the heavenly bodies seems to be alluded to in Gen. vi, when the sons of God saw the daughters of men that they were fair, and assaulted them. Out of these unnatural unions sprang the giants. We may reasonably connect the sons of God with the stars on the basis of Job xxxviii. 7:

> When the morning stars sang together, and all the sons of God shouted for joy.

The spiritual enemies of man are thus powers that should be his servants, and Christ's final victory over them will mean their return to their proper status and function. When Christ as the Man becomes lord over all things in heaven, on earth, and under the earth, these are not annihilated, but reduced to their proper service to—the Man, and to mankind, of which he is the head, in him.

One or perhaps two exceptions may be made here. One is death. Death is an enemy, and death will be brought to nothing (I Cor. xv. 26). This is because death is not a perverted and rebellious servant, but God's sentence on sin (Rom. vi. 23). The other possible exception is sin itself, which sometimes is almost personified (*e.g.* Rom. vii. 8, 13, 17). Sin is actually, even when personified, rebellion itself, and in the event of reconciliation it naturally comes to an end. It may be, however, that even here there is a positive word to say. As the Rabbis recognized that even the evil *yēṣer* had its value[1]—without it men would not have families, build houses and cities, and so on—so sin is the perversion of an urge within human nature that can be put to good use. It is right that man should wish to be a lord; wrong only when he uses his lordship in the wrong direction. The desire which the law under sin unfortunately evokes is a

---

[1] See p. 16, n. 2.

perversion of the love which the law commands.

The victory of Christ becomes complete at his *parousia*, and this consummation is eagerly awaited not only by men but also by the lower creation (Rom. viii. 19-22), for all creation has been subjected to ματαιότης—not simply vanity, but false spiritual beings whose rule is corruption (φθορά)—and therefore awaits liberation at the hands of Christ.

Throughout this book I have tried to distinguish between the two needful elements in redemption—the cosmic act of deliverance, and the inner anthropological rectification of man's existence in the sight of God. It is only as we continue to keep them clearly in mind that Paul's paradoxical language (quoted above) about universal and limited salvation can be resolved. The act of deliverance has been taken in hand, and will be completed, with reference to the cosmos; there is no other way in which it could be done at all. It does not, however, follow from this that the inner rectification will be the destiny of every single man. 'In Christ shall all be made alive', since Christ has not overcome, and will not overcome, death on behalf of this or that man, but on behalf of Man. It was as the Man that he died and rose, and it was for man that he died and rose. But resurrection and life are the mark of the new age, and those who continue to live in the old age continue to live in death. The renewed cosmos no more guarantees their faith and obedience than the as yet unfallen cosmos guaranteed Adam's. To say this is not to rehabilitate the freedom of the human will to achieve or to reject salvation for itself. God uses the paradox of the will as he uses the paradox of time in order to manifest the way in which he works. The paradox of time means that in this world, upon the bank and shoal of time, we are the inhabitants of two ages at the same time. By faith we live in the world of the resurrection with and in Christ; but in the world in which we walk by sight we live in death, from which there is no escape and no release. The paradox of the will means that in these circumstances it is declared to man that Christ is risen from the dead, and that he, the hearer, is himself incorporated in this resurrected humanity; that the forgiveness of sins is free, and that justification is to be had by faith only. There are some who do and there are others who do not close with this declaration, and the existence of these 'elect' and 'reprobate' manifests the freedom of God to act in grace, independently of the merit, virtue, or religion of men. We cannot say more than that in Jesus Christ we see the fate of the old humanity and the birth of the new, since he is himself the representative Man. How each man finds himself in him is mystery, and never prospectively revealed. Moreover, even the terms 'elect' and 'reprobate', which have just been used, do not denote fixed categories. They belong to the period of eschatological flux, and come under the rule of 'as if not'. The man who in his devotion to Christ feels himself to be 'elect' must regard his election as if it were not election; it is entirely uncertain, and he must constantly discipline himself lest he become 'reprobate' (cf. I Cor. ix. 27). There is no man so evidently 'reprobate' that his reprobation must not be regarded as if it were not reprobation; it is entirely uncertain, and to him also, to him especially, the good news of what has happened to him and all mankind in Jesus Christ must be proclaimed.

The Pauline conception is delicately balanced, and impossible to express in simple and rigid terms. Its delicacy stands out most clearly when it is compared with the heavy-handed attempts of later Christian generations to hammer Paul's theology into dogmatics. At every point one can detect a hardening, a solidifying, of the mobile and dynamic thought that we have now, from one special angle, examined. Predestination becomes a rigid imposition of a numerical class-distinction instead of the wrestling of the absolute freedom of God with the limited freedom of man; eschatology becomes 'the doctrine of the last things' instead of a definition and determination of the present; the Church and the world begin to glare at each other across an iron curtain; the sacraments become *opera operata*, medicines of immortality, mediating and guaranteeing salvation, instead of exciting personal encounters taking place within the context of the divine family; 'ministry' comes to mean an order of spiritual bureaucrats, who look after the souls of the laymen who provide their bread and butter, instead of the common activity of the *laos* (people) of God. The history of the second century is enough to show how easily and how quickly these perversions and degenerations can take place; and the whole of Church History stands as a witness to the Church's permanent need of the Jewish Doctor of the Gentiles.

# INDEXES

## I. NEW TESTAMENT REFERENCES

## II. SUBJECTS

## III. MODERN AUTHORS